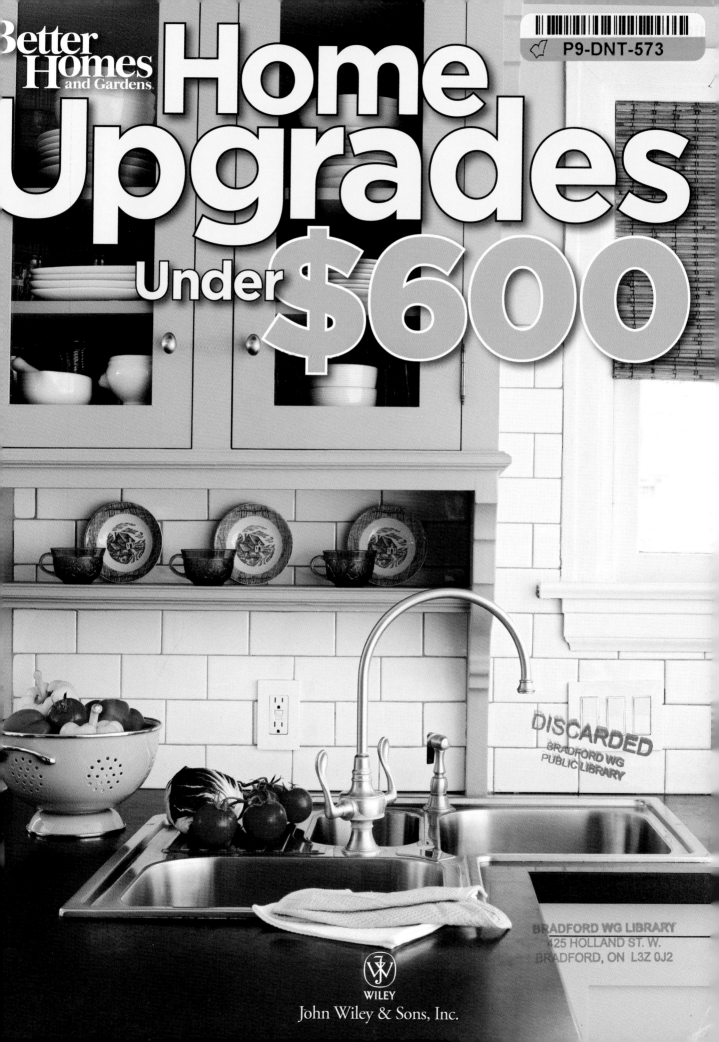

Better Homes and Gardens

Home Upgrades Under $600

P9-DNT-573

DISCARDED
BRADFORD WG
PUBLIC LIBRARY

BRADFORD WG LIBRARY
425 HOLLAND ST. W.
BRADFORD, ON L3Z 0J2

WILEY
John Wiley & Sons, Inc.

Note to the Readers:

Due to differing conditions, tools, and individual skills, John Wiley & Sons, Inc., assumes no responsibility for any damages, injuries suffered, or losses incurred as a result of following the information published in this book. Before beginning any project, review the instructions carefully, and if any doubts or questions remain, consult local experts or authorities. Because codes and regulations vary greatly, you always should check with authorities to ensure that your project complies with all applicable local codes and regulations. Always read and observe all of the safety precautions provided by manufacturers of any tools, equipment, or supplies, and follow all accepted safety procedures.

Sometimes the process of home improvement gets stalled because the next step is too big—calling for more time, skill, or money than we have at our disposal.

That's a good time to take a second look. Look at the big picture and ponder, "What *can* I do right now, with the resources I have today?" You might surprise yourself with the options in front of you. There are dozens of valuable, worthwhile, satisfying improvements you can make in an evening or a weekend, all with a modest budget. A series of any of these projects can become simple steps toward realizing your home's potential.

This book is about those opportunities, genuine upgrades you can make now. You'll gain a fresh perspective on your home and a fresh appreciation for your own abilities.

—The Editors

Home Upgrades Under $600

Contents

Chapter 5   Beautifying Windows & Doors   114

Chapter 6   Finding Storage Solutions   130

Chapter 7   Improving Lighting & Wiring   144

Chapter 8   Adding Yard Improvements   160

Chair railing and wall frames of the same material are simple projects that give this room a casual elegance.

Fresh colors like this flirtatious pink have powers to transform. Learn about painting in Chapter 1.

Just about any bathroom can be made new-looking by replacing the sink and medicine cabinet, then adding some lights and a few nice shelves.

Sumptuous trim is created with of simple parts. We'll show you easy it really is.

Engineered wood flooring can be installed in a day, with no sanding or staining.

Seeing the Opportunity
for all areas of the house

Take a fresh look at your home and look for its potential.
You'll find inspiring examples on these pages—
plus instructions for many other projects throughout this book.

Kitchen cabinets with simple, straight lines are ideal candidates for painting. Check out our cabinet painting instructions to get professional-looking results.

This intriguing room had coarse, unfinished floor and ceiling surfaces. The owners chose to simply paint them, spending their money instead on new windows and glassed doors.

Bamboo blinds provide dappled shade and can be raised to show off the spacious windows.

This room's palette of whites emphasizes differences in texture. Sticking with one light color makes a room feel open and bright.

A playful and colorful palette of textiles breathes life into this charming space, where a collection of globes overhead echo tones in the rug.

This earth-toned outdoor floor is made of hexagonal Saltillo tiles mortared onto a concrete slab.

Low-voltage outdoor lighting is an inexpensive way to dress up a home's exterior and improve safety at night.

Low walls of stacked stones are capped with bluestone slabs, which are mortared on top. Smaller yet elegant stone projects can be achieved on modest budgets.

A few decorative touches transform this sunny wall into a focal point of the backyard. Stepping stones create an inviting path to other features in the yard, and smaller stones define an oasis of tiny flowers in the center.

A simple wire trellis supports this stunning arc of lush climbing roses and serves as an inviting entrance to a sitting area in the back of the yard. Flat stones are stacked to make a low wall for a raised bed, and are also laid on the lawn to create a steppingstone path.

CHAPTER 1

To be inside a house is to be surrounded by walls. Walls define spaces, and in that role they can be comforting or confining. They offer the biggest and easiest opportunity to give any room a welcome new style.

In this chapter we'll show you ways to bring fresh character to your walls. Color, texture, pattern, and trimwork give you virtually unlimited choices.

Where to start? The entryway is the first thing visitors will see when they enter your home, so make sure it welcomes them in style. If you can't change the whole space, concentrate on high-impact items. An entryway offers a good opportunity to focus on architectural details—moldings, for example. If they're present, play them up with a fresh finish. If they're absent, we'll show you how to add them.

We start this chapter with paint, because color is basic to the way a room makes us feel. Resist the urge to jump too quickly into a painting project. You'll thank yourself for years if you spend time choosing just the right colors and if you employ the correct techniques to achieve great results.

In addition to paint, we'll show a variety of trim treatments, including chair rail, crown molding, wainscoting, and paneling. All of these can be installed by a do-it-yourselfer with basic carpentry skills, some decent tools, and the willingness to work carefully and patiently. In most cases, you can transform a room in less than a day by applying trim.

Enlivening Walls

Painting Walls and Trim

Almost every real estate pro will tell you that the quickest and most cost-effective way to raise the value of a home is to cover walls and ceilings with a fresh coat of attractive paint. And a good paint job will also raise your spirits and make your home a more satisfying place to be.

Painting is an excellent do-it-yourself project. Just don't underestimate the time, attention to detail, and prep time needed for a quality job. Follow the tips on the following pages to produce painted rooms with crisp lines and smooth or consistently textured surfaces.

MATERIALS & TOOLS:

- Sponge and detergent or deglossing liquid
- Wall and trim paint
- Brushes, rollers, and roller sleeves
- Roller extension pole
- Paint tray
- Spackle, painter's caulk, and wood filler
- Taping blade
- Hand sander and 100-grit sandpaper
- Drop cloths and rosin (kraft) paper
- Painter's tape
- Razor-blade scraper

Choosing the Colors

Colors that look great in the store can be disappointing once they're on the walls. Here are some tips to help you choose colors that set just the mood you're after:

- Consider the color combinations suggested by paint companies. Every home center or paint store has brochures and cards depicting color schemes—a wall color, a trim color, and an accent color. For a wider range of choices, go to websites such as BHG.com and sites from various paint brands, and look for a tab that shows rooms with colors. Once you have found a combination that suits you, you can order the exact colors using the manufacturer's names and tint numbers.

- If you find your perfect colors in a publication, take the page to your paint source. The printing process often skews the color of rooms, so buying the same paint may not get the color you see pictured. Instead, have your paint source scan the page and match the color that appeals to you there.

- Think of your home as having its own palette. A certain amount of continuity helps anchor the overall effect. For instance, all or most of the wood trim may be painted the same color—a color that will coordinate with the rest of a room; a shade of off-white with a little yellow for warmth is often a good choice.

- Pay attention to the glosses. Flat paint is usually the best choice for walls because it downplays surface imperfections. Semigloss paint is often used for trim because it better resists smudging, but it will also show underlying blemishes more clearly. You may prefer to paint your trim with less-glossy satin or eggshell paint.

- One strategy is to paint transition areas—halls and entryways—with deep and intense colors, and then lighten the walls as you move through the home toward rooms with the most natural daylight.

- Follow the 60-30-10 rule: The room's dominant color (including furnishings as well as walls) should be 60 percent of its total color. Then 30 percent should be a secondary color—often trim, and perhaps upholstery. Finally, 10 percent can be accent colors, including decorative touches like pillows.

Prepping Walls and Trim

Paint does not hide bumps, dings, and other imperfections in walls and trim. Take time to smooth them out before painting. And take steps to ensure that the new paint will stick to the old. Remove all switch and outlet cover plates, and cover the switches and outlets with tape.

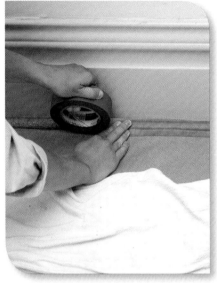

No matter how skilled you are, paint will spatter. Most painting pros spread drop cloths before they start, and so should you. A safe choice is to tape rosin paper to the floor, tape any trim you do not want to paint, and then throw a cloth drop cloth over the paper.

Wash walls with a mild detergent solution or a deglossing liquid. This removes greases that can keep the new paint from sticking to the wall. If you suspect that your existing paint is oil-based, sand the entire surface, and apply a coat of primer before painting.

Fill small depressions with spackle. Apply with a taping blade, first pushing the spackle into the depression, then scraping lightly to remove most of the excess.

Fill small holes with spackle. For larger holes, or on surfaces that will often be handled, use wood filler, which is stronger. If trim has developed "alligator skin" or other surface flaws, scrape and sand the old paint first.

TIP: THE IMPORTANCE OF PRIMER

- If the existing paint is water-based (latex or acrylic) and in good shape, with no stains, you can usually simply paint over it with the new paint. However, there are times when it is best to apply primer first.

- If you are not sure whether the existing paint is water- or oil-based, scrape off a chip and break it with your fingers. If the chip bends a bit before it snaps, it is probably water-based. If it cracks without bending, it is probably oil-based. In that case, be sure to apply a primer coat before painting.

- If there are stains on the wall—either localized or generalized stains from smoking—apply a stain-killing primer before painting. If you don't, the stains may bleed through even three or more coats of paint.

- A paint store or home center can tint the primer for you—usually at no charge—so it nearly matches the color of the finish paint. This can save you from having to apply two coats of paint instead of one.

Painting Walls and Trim

(Continued from previous page)

STEP-BY-STEP >>> Painting a Ceiling

❶ In general, when you paint with two colors that will abut, fill corners with the lighter color, then cut the straight line using the darker color. So when painting a light-colored ceiling, start by giving the corners a generous brushing of the ceiling color. Don't worry about getting paint on the wall; you will cover it later. Paint about a 3-inch strip of the ceiling perimeter.

❷ Screw an extension pole onto a paint roller. Pour ceiling paint into a paint tray, and load the roller (see step 2 below). Roll paint onto the ceiling, starting with a zigzag pattern, then filling in the gaps. Run the roller within an inch or so of the walls, so you cover the brushed line from step 1, but avoid touching the wall with the roller. Keep your eye on the places where roller passes overlap, and finish with light strokes to avoid noticeable lines.

❸ Allow the ceiling paint to dry, then look closely for "holidays" (missing spots) and irregularities, especially near the corners. Once you are satisfied with the ceiling paint job, dip a brush into the wall paint, and scrape the paint off one side of the brush. Work carefully to make a straight line at the top of the wall, where it meets the ceiling. With a bit of practice you can achieve neat-looking corners, but you may need to touch up some places with ceiling paint.

Painting a Wall

❶ Brush-paint the areas where the roller cannot reach. Where two walls of the same color meet, apply plenty of paint to the corner. Where a wall abuts another wall or trim that will be painted another color, apply the lighter-colored paint to the corner.

❷ Pour paint into a paint tray until it starts to come up onto the tray's sloping surface. Screw an extension pole onto the roller. Dip the roller's sleeve lightly into the paint and roll it back a bit, and repeat until paint covers the entire roller sleeve. Fill the sleeve with a good coating of paint, but not so much that it drips.

❸ Work in an area about 3 feet by 4 feet. Roll paint in a zigzag pattern, as shown, then go back and use nearly straight up-and-down motions to fill in the voids. Quickly go over the area, taking care to remove any obvious paint lines.

Painting Trim Freehand

❶ With practice you can learn to apply neat lines of paint along edges freehand style. Dip a high-quality brush about an inch into the paint, and wipe off one side. Apply the paint side of the brush to the trim an inch or so away from the corner, and move toward the corner as you run the brush with a smooth, nonstop stroke.

❷ Once the paint has dried, you can remove paint from glass easily. Use a razor blade, or better, a small hand tool that houses a razor blade. Place the blade on the glass and scrape gently up to the wood. You may also need to scrape while holding the blade perpendicular to the glass and alongside the edge of the wood.

TIPS: PAINT LIKE A PRO

• If an underlying stain keeps bleeding through, or if a spackled area appears a different color after painting, apply stain-killing primer to the spot.

• Move your ladder often, rather than leaning precariously to reach out-of-the-way areas. This is easier on your back and will ensure a neater job.

• When painting a door or other wide wood surface, paint the edges with a brush, then go over the entire surface with a roller.

• A roller sleeve with a thick ½-inch nap will hold lots of paint, but it will also produce a pronounced stipple—a pattern of low bumps. If you want a smooth surface, use a sleeve with a ¼-inch nap. Many people choose a middle course and opt for a ⅜-inch nap.

Painting Trim with Tape

❶ For crisp lines without a steady, deft hand, rely on painter's tape. The trade-off: It adds some time and expense. Hold tape fairly taut as you apply it, to produce straight lines. Smooth the edges with your finger or a putty knife to ensure that paint cannot ooze under.

❷ Apply ample paint so you don't have to do a second coat. Where possible, run your brush from the tape to the wood, rather than toward the tape. That reduces the risk of getting paint under the taped edge.

❸ Remove the tape within an hour of painting. (Latex or acrylic paint continues to harden after drying to the touch.) Peel the tape away from the wood, and roll up the tape as you go; some underlying paint may still be wet.

Taped Horizontal Stripes

Contemporary and adventurous, horizontal stripes make a bold statement in any room. Painting stripes one or two tones darker than the base coat in this living room takes a basic beige wall from boring to dynamic. Unlike vertical stripes, which lead the eye up and create the illusion of vertical space, horizontal stripes lead the eye along the wall and appear to expand the space outward. Paint only one wall for a focal point in the room or wrap stripes around corners to include two or more walls. When designing your stripe width and color arrangement, sketch your ideas on graph paper to help visualize your plan. For an overall pattern of horizontal stripes, widths from 14 to 20 inches give the most pleasing effect. Use varying stripe widths to add borders, simulate architectural elements, or create a more intricate pattern on a focal-point wall.

Mask ceiling, baseboards, and trim with painter's tape. Paint the entire wall in the light base-coat color. Paint two coats if necessary. Leave the tape on; let the paint dry overnight.

To divide the room into stripes of equal width, first measure the height of each wall in inches. Next divide the total wall height by the desired stripe width to determine the number of stripes. The stripes shown here measure 16 inches, but you may choose a different stripe width to get the look you desire.

MATERIALS & TOOLS:

- Base-coat paint
- Stripe-color paint
- Tape measure
- Level with printed ruler
- Low-tack painter's tape
- Mini roller
- Drop cloth
- Stir sticks
- Paint tray
- Standard roller frame with 9-inch roller cover
- Graph paper
- Colored pencil
- Chip brush

STEP-BY-STEP >>>

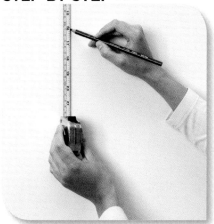

❶ **Starting at the ceiling** use a tape measure and colored pencil to make a series of measurement marks moving vertically down the wall.

❷ **Use a long level to draw horizontal lines,** connecting the marks at each stripe interval. The level will ensure that the lines stay horizontal and parallel to one another. Periodically check the stripes to make sure they remain parallel and even.

3 **Apply low-tack painter's tape** along the outside edges of each alternating stripe, pressing down firmly on the inner edges of the tape.

4 **Use the chip brush to repaint** the base coat color along the taped edges of each stripe. This seals the tape to the wall and helps prevent the top coat of paint from bleeding underneath. Allow to dry.

5 **Use the mini roller to paint the stripes.** Paint two coats if necessary to ensure solid coverage, letting the paint dry between coats.

6 **After the paint has set up slightly** and begins to dry, it loses its shiny, wet look. This is the time to carefully remove the tape by pulling outward from the wall at a 90-degree angle. Allow paint to dry.

Silk Strié

The shimmering reflective quality of silk fabric imparts elegance and sophistication to a home's decor. And the opulent look of silk wall coverings can be achieved with ease at a fraction of the cost of silk.

Pearlescent glaze and a special strié brush are the secrets to this elegant faux-fabric technique. The pearlescent quality of the glaze produces a softly shimmering patina. The strié brush has long, soft bristles that create very fine, soft, and slightly uneven streaks when pulled through the glaze top coat to simulate the look of raw silk. If you wish to avoid investing in a strié brush, you can create a similar look with an inexpensive wallpaper brush, but the streaks will be more pronounced.

This elegant finish adds upscale luxury to formal living and dining rooms or to private spaces such as bedrooms or baths. During the day, sunlight playing off the walls will radiate a warm glow, and soft lamplight or candlelight will enhance the effect in the evening hours.

MATERIALS & TOOLS:

- Level with printed ruler
- 2-inch-wide low-tack painter's tape
- Pearlescent glaze medium
- Strié brush
- Drop cloth
- Stir sticks
- Paint tray
- Standard roller frame with 9-inch roller cover
- 2-inch tapered trim brush
- Tape measure
- Colored pencil
- Plastic container with printed measurements
- Large plastic bucket
- Lint-free cotton cloths

STEP-BY-STEP >>>

① To lay out the panels, use a tape measure and colored pencil to measure and mark all the walls with an upper and lower mark for each panel. Then use a long level to draw in vertical lines from ceiling to baseboard, connecting upper and lower marks at each panel. The level will ensure that the lines stay vertical and parallel to one another.

② Since every other strip is painted the first day and the remaining strips are painted the next day, tape off alternating sections with low-tack painter's tape.

3 **Use a trim brush** to trim with the glaze mixture along the ceiling and baseboard of the first taped-off panel. Then use a well-saturated roller to apply glaze to the remainder of the panel. Quickly roll long vertical strokes from ceiling to baseboard across the entire width of the panel to even out the glaze.

4 **Draw the strié brush through the glaze** from top to bottom in one continuous motion, creating a vertical pattern in the wet glaze. If you must use a ladder to reach the ceiling, make a few dry runs to practice stepping down the ladder as you pull the brush through the glaze. Wipe the excess glaze off the brush with a lint-free cloth and repeat until the panel is complete.

5 **Remove the vertical strips** of painter's tape immediately after dragging and while the glaze is still wet. Complete the first series of panels and let them dry overnight before taping and painting the final series, repeating steps 2–4. To abut the seams, place the tape on top of the dried glaze along the edge where the sections meet.

TIP: CHOOSING PAINT COLORS

- When choosing paint colors use a neutral hue or one in the same color family as the top glaze coat for best results.

- To reduce the amount of metallic shimmer in the final finish, add clear glaze medium to the glaze mixture.

Wall Decals

Here's a quick and fun way to add decorative pizzazz. Wall decals are available from paint stores and online sources (search for "wall decals"). Some (like those shown on the page opposite) come as single large images; others, like those shown in the steps below, come as ensembles of smaller decals. Many cost less than $50. They are self-adhesive, and stick readily to painted walls and ceilings. Once you want to change the look of a room, they easily peel off with no damage to the paint.

Decals can also be applied to glass, plastic, or metal surfaces. These decals attach firmly and evenly on a wall that is smooth. If yours has a textured surface, results will not be as satisfactory.

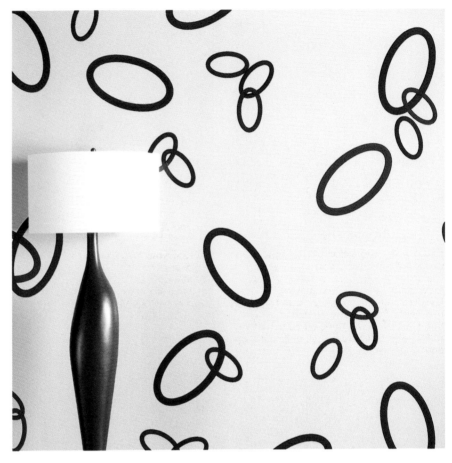

Decals have a white backing that covers the adhesive side on the back, and a clear transfer sheet in front to allow you to squeegee without damaging the decal. Some include a squeegee tool for applying the decal.

MATERIALS & TOOLS:

- Wall decals
- Graph paper and pencil
- Tape measure
- Hard rubber squeegee
- Painter's tape

STEP-BY-STEP >>>

❶ Using graph paper, sketch out a design to determine the placement of the decals. With that as a guide, test the pattern by attaching the decals to the wall with painter's tape.

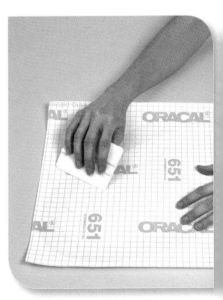

❷ Lay each decal face-down on a smooth surface. Press firmly as you scrape with the squeegee along the entire surface, to make sure the decal is securely affixed to the transfer paper.

❸ Carefully peel off the backing to expose the adhesive side. Don't allow the decal to fold back on itself, or you may create wrinkles that cannot be removed. Gently position the decal on the wall with the transfer sheet facing out. Starting in the middle and working outward, rub the squeegee over the entire surface.

❹ Using your fingernail or a knife, gently pry the transfer paper off the wall at a corner, then pull at an angle. If the decal starts to come off the wall, re-squeegee the transfer paper as in step 3, and try again.

❺ Continue applying decals in the same way. If one decal overlays another, take special care when peeling the transfer paper so that neither of the decals lifts off the wall.

Applying Large Graphics

Large decals like the one shown in the photos here come in single rolled-up sheets. To apply a large wall decal like the faux headboard above, tape it in place at the corners, making sure there are no creases or bubbles. Then apply pieces of tape in the middle to act as a hinge, so you can work on one side,

then the other. Remove the corner pieces of tape from one side and pull half the graphic away from the wall. Working with a helper, remove the backing, taking care not to wrinkle the decal. When you reach the middle of the decal, use a knife to cut the paper and remove it. Gently roll the

decal back onto the wall, taking care to avoid bubbles and wrinkles. Press in place with your hand, then with the squeegee. Remove the other corner pieces of tape, as well as the hinge pieces, and repeat the process for the other half of the decal.

Chair Rail

A chair rail is a horizontal molding that runs all the way around a room at a height of about 32 inches above the floor. It is quick and easy to install, and can make a dramatic difference in a room, especially if you choose to paint or wallpaper the area below the chair rail differently from the wall above.

You could simply buy pieces of chair rail molding and attach them directly to the wall. The steps on this page show applying four pieces—a support piece, a top and bottom trim piece, and chair rail molding—for a more dramatic effect.

Depending on the wall colors you choose, chair rail can perk up a room or make it look more stately.

MATERIALS & TOOLS:

- Chair rail molding, and perhaps other moldings
- Stud finder
- Tape measure
- Level
- Miter saw
- Wood glue
- Hammer and nail set or power nailer with finish nails
- Chalk line
- Wood filler
- Sandpaper

STEP-BY-STEP >>>

❶ At wall corners or vertical molding pieces, measure up from the floor 32 inches and make a light mark on the wall. Snap chalk lines to establish guidelines. Use a stud finder or drive test holes to locate the wall studs, and mark their locations lightly.

❷ Cut the support pieces to fit snugly. Align each piece with the marks on the wall, and check with a level; you may need to deviate from the chalk line a bit. Drive nails into studs to attach the support pieces.

❸ Cut small pieces of cove or other molding to fit along the top and bottom edges of the support pieces. To attach them, first apply a bead of glue to the joint along the wall and the support piece. Position the molding and drive nails into studs.

❹ Cut pieces of chair rail molding to fit, and nail them to the support piece. Where the chair rail meets a vertical molding and is thicker than the vertical molding, mark it and make a 45-degree bevel cut for a neat appearance.

Wall Frames

A series of neatly spaced wall frames around a room can really mark it off as a special place with old-world charm. Wall frames may be of various heights. If you combine wall frames with chair rail, you may want to install short wall frames below the chair rail and taller frames directly above. If there is no chair rail, you can install tall wall frames, with their tops the same distance below the ceiling as the bottoms are above the base molding.

Make the frames out of molding that is 1½ to 2 inches wide. If you want the frames to be a different color than the wall, give the molding two coats of paint before cutting it; then you will only need to touch up the corners after installation. Or install the frames unpainted and simply paint them the same color as the wall.

This project takes much more time and materials than a simple chair rail, but it also does more to transform a room.

MATERIALS & TOOLS:
- Molding
- Plywood for the template
- Tape measure and pencil
- 1½-inch nails
- Hammer and nail set or power nailer
- Power miter saw or hand miter box with saw
- Hammer and nail set or power nailer
- Chalk line
- Stud finder
- Framing square
- Wood filler and wood glue

Formulas to Calculate Wall Frame Width and Spacing

Formula A: This formula calculates the spacing between frames when the frame width is known. Decide how many frames are to fit on the wall, then calculate the space (S) between the frames and between the frames and other moldings or wall corners using the following formula:

$$S = WW - (FW \times F) \div (F + 1)$$

WW = Width of wall
FW = Width of one frame
F = Number of frames

Example:
WW = 108″, FW = 22″, F = 4
S = (108″ - 22″ x 4) ÷ 5
S = (108″ - 88″) ÷ 5
S = 20″ ÷ 5
S = 4″ space between frames

Formula B: This formula calculates the frame width when spacing between the frames is known. Decide how many frames you want to fit on the wall, then calculate the frame width (FW) using the following formula:

$$FW = WW - [S \times (F + 1)] \div F$$

WW = Width of wall
F = Number of frames
S = Space between frames

Example:
WW = 84″, S = 4″, F = 3
FW = 84″ – [4″ x (3+1)] ÷ 3
FW = 84″ – [4″ x 4] ÷ 3
FW = 84″ – 16″ ÷ 3
FW = 68″ ÷ 3
FW = 22⅔″ frame width

Wall Frames

(Continued from previous page)

Laying Out Wall Frames

Measure your walls and existing moldings carefully, and make a scale drawing of each wall. Make several copies of the drawings so you can experiment with various frame arrangements.

Determine how many frames you want. A frame below a window or above a door should be the same width as the window's or door's casing. Estimate the length of each frame, then use Formula A at the bottom of page 25 to calculate the spacing. Adjust the frame height and spacing for the most pleasing effect.

On a wall that includes a door, the spacing often works out differently for the panels on each side of the door. To accommodate that difference, it is usually best to vary the width of the frames. You can also vary the spacing between the frames, but not by more than an inch or so; spacing variations are much more noticeable than frame width variations. For example, our wall for this project included a door. We used Formula B to determine

spacing on frames for the larger area of the wall. On the other side of the door, we made each frame a fraction of an inch wider, preferring that option over increasing the 4-inch spaces between the frames.

Building and Installing Frames

Though you can use a hammer, a pneumatic power nailer is recommended for this project. With a power nailer, you can hold the frame pieces in perfect alignment with one hand as you drive a nail with the other hand, and the parts won't jump around as they will when hand nailing.

Choose molding that is in keeping with the character of the room. You may want to match the profiles of existing moldings in your room, or make frames that contrast sharply in profile.

Still unsure about the selection of molding to use? Buy one piece and make a test frame that you can lean against your wall to see if you like the effect.

TIP: CUTTING MOLDING

Use a hand miter saw and miter box or a power miter saw to cut the molding pieces to 45 degrees at each end. To cut a number of pieces to the same length, make a simple jig like the one shown, with a screwed-down piece of wood to hold the molding at the correct length.

STEP-BY-STEP >>>

❶ Mark a top or bottom guideline. Measure up or down from the nearest existing horizontal molding or ceiling and make a light mark at each end of a wall. Snap a chalk line between the marks to create a layout line.

❷ Mark for vertical lines. Mark the top corners of each wall frame on the chalk line. Make two guides from scrap pieces of wood: one the interval width between frames, and one the width to the chair rail.

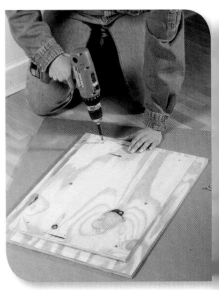

❸ Make a template. Cut a piece of ½-inch plywood to the dimensions of the frame (that is, the outside dimension minus two times the width of the molding you are using). Attach it to a larger piece of plywood so the bottom piece extends at least 1½ inches beyond the template on all sides.

TIP: USING A SPACER

- To ensure that all the spaces are consistent in width, make a T-spacer: Rip-cut a piece about 16 inches long to the width of the space, and fasten a cross piece to one end. Place this spacer between frames when fastening them.

- When you run up against a window or door, adjust the size of the frames, not the spacing between them. Use the same spacer to maintain consistent spacing.

④ Assemble the frame. Miter-cut the pieces, and test the fit around the template. Apply glue to one of the miters. Holding two pieces tightly together, drive a nail in each direction to fasten the joint tightly. Repeat for all four joints.

⑤ Nail the frames to the wall. Use a stud finder or exploratory nails to locate wall studs, and make light marks on the wall to indicate their centers. Once you are certain of the alignment, drive nails through the top piece of the frame securely into the studs.

⑥ Nail the sides. At the sides you will probably not be able to drive nails into studs. Drive these nails at an angle, which will provide a bit of grip when fastening to drywall only.

⑦ Set the nails and fill the holes with wood filler. Caulk any gaps on the inside and outside. Allow the filler to dry, and sand smooth. Prime and paint.

Crown Molding

Installing crown molding is well within the reach of someone with basic carpentry skills. You can cut the pieces using a hand miter box and attach them using a hammer, but a power miter saw and a power finishing nailer make it easier to produce neat results. The following pages show installing molding that will be painted, allowing you to fill imperfections with wood putty or caulk. Installing moldings that will be stained is a much less forgiving task.

Plan all the cuts carefully. Usually it makes sense to first install a square-cut piece on a wall with two inside corners, then add the other pieces, which must be cope-cut, as shown opposite. If the room has an outside corner, cope-cut the pieces on one end first, then cut for the outside corner, as shown on page 31. If you have a bump-out, some pieces will need to be miter-cut or cope-cut on each end. "Sneak up" on the correct length: cut them a bit long, hold in place to learn the precise size, then cut shorter as needed.

Choose moldings that fit with the overall design of the house. Wide, ornate ogee molding has an old-world elegance; bed moldings lend themselves more to a cottage feel; and cove moldings spruce up more modern-looking rooms.

MATERIALS & TOOLS:

- Crown molding
- Two-by lumber that can be rip-cut to make backer strips
- Tape measure
- Hand or power miter saw
- Framing square
- Coping saw
- Power nailer or hammer and finishing nails
- Drill
- Caulk and wood filler

Crown moldings range in width from 4⅝" for the widest ogee to 1½" for the narrowest bed and cove moldings.

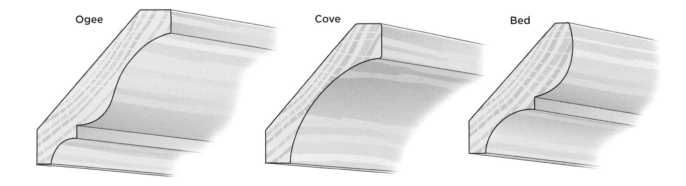

Ogee   Cove   Bed

STEP-BY-STEP >>>

① **Using a miter saw,** cut the first piece at right angles to fit snugly in the room. Drive nails to attach it.

② **Cut the next piece longer** than it needs to be. Position it next to the first, and draw a rough line angling up from the bottom corner. Label the top of the molding as shown.

③ **Set a miter saw to cut** at 45 degrees. Position the "top" side of the molding on bottom, as shown, and make the cut.

④ **Hold the piece you have just cut** in position to confirm that you have cut it at the correct angle.

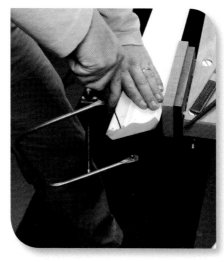

⑤ **Using a coping saw,** cut along the line where the cut meets the face of the molding. Angle the coping saw back to create a sharp edge.

⑥ **Press the cut piece in place** and note any high spots that are keeping the joint from being tight. File or cut away high spots. Measure and cut the other end of the molding, and nail it in place.

Filling Gaps

Before you paint, apply caulk to any gaps between the molding and the wall or ceiling. Wipe the excess with your finger, or with a tightly balled-up moist rag. Fill nail holes with wood putty.

Crown Molding

(Continued from previous page)

Backer Strips

If the ceiling and walls are flat and at perfect 90-degree angles to each other, you can simply nail crown molding to the top plate of the wall framing or to the ceiling joists. However, if you are installing wide molding and the ceiling and walls are less than perfect, it will be difficult to keep the molding straight as you work. The solution is to cut and install backer strips.

1. Hold a piece of the molding against a framing square to determine the height and width of the space behind the molding.

2. Using a table saw, cut backer strips from 2x4 lumber. Most often, the blade should be set to cut at a 38-degree bevel.

3. Drive screws to attach the backer strips to framing in the wall.

4. The backer strip keeps the crown molding at a consistent angle, ensuring tight joints.

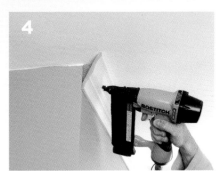

Scarf Joint

If you don't have a piece of molding long enough to reach across a wall, you'll need to splice two pieces together. You could simply flat-cut each, but the resulting butt joint will be obvious. A scarf joint, with both pieces cut at 45 degrees, makes a neater appearance.

Cut the first piece at 45 degrees, as shown. Nail it in place. Cut the other end of the second piece as needed (with a flat cut, coped cut, or outside miter). Hold the piece in place or measure from the corner and mark where this piece meets the long tip of the installed molding. Draw a rough line indicating the angle of the scarf cut. Cut at 45 degrees, and test the fit. Once you are satisfied, apply glue to both ends and drive nails to attach the second piece. Sand away any irregularities.

STEP-BY-STEP >>> Installing an Outside Corner

➊ **Use a framing square** to check whether the outside corner is square. If the corner is less than 90 degrees, the miter cuts will be less than 45 degrees; if it is more than 90 degrees, the miter cuts will be more than 45 degrees. Test-cut scrap pieces of molding until you find the correct angle. (You need to cut both pieces at the same angle, or the joint will look sloppy.)

➋ **Cut the other end of the piece so it fits snugly** (often, this will be a cope-cut, as shown on page 29).

➌ **Put the moldings in place** one at a time and mark where the corner meets at the bottom. Draw a rough line indicating the direction of the angled cut.

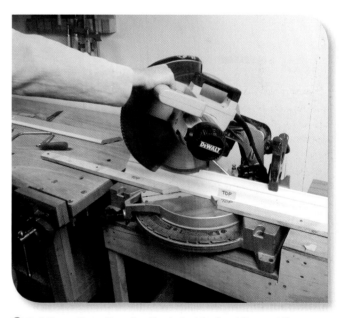

➍ **Cut the miters.** To miter the left side, feed the molding from the right, with the top on the saw bed. Miter 45 degrees to the left. Hold both pieces in place, and check for high spots that keep the joint from being tight. You may need to slightly adjust the cut, or file the back side of the joint in places. Drive nails to attach both pieces to the wall and ceiling.

Wainscoting

Wainscoting is basically solid-wood paneling installed to a height of about 4 feet. Its original purpose was to protect walls from damage, but nowadays it is a sought-after decorative touch. Traditionally wainscoting is most commonly installed in a dining room, but it's equally at home in a child's bedroom, a family room, or even a bathroom. In pantries, entryways, and hallways it can serve its original practical purpose, especially if you have dogs or rambunctious children.

Beadboard and V-board are strips, commonly 3½ inches wide, that fit together via tongues and grooves. Beadboard has a double groove for a more ornate look; V-board is simpler in design. You can also buy plywood sheets milled to look like beadboard.

Wainscoting is usually a welcome touch that is most attractive in small doses. Use it in a few areas or rooms only, so it gives a room a special quality. Softwood wainscoting, usually made of pine or hem-fir, is a good choice for a cottage-style or informal room. You can lightly stain and seal it, or paint it. For a more formal look, buy oak, cherry, or other wainscoting materials. These are more expensive, and need to be installed carefully.

MATERIALS & TOOLS:

- Beadboard or V-board
- Nosing or panel trim for top of wainscoting
- Plywood strips for backing
- Compass and pencil
- Drill and screws
- Hammer or power nailer and finish nails
- Construction adhesive and caulk gun
- Level
- Power saw and jigsaw

Beadboard Wainscoting Options

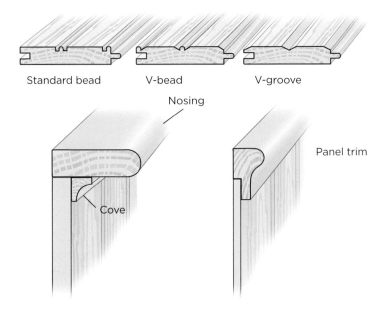

Standard bead   V-bead   V-groove

Nosing

Cove

Panel trim

Prepping the Wall

Each wainscoting board should be anchored firmly to the wall. However, you will not be able to attach most of the boards to studs, which are usually 16 inches apart. At the bottom, you should be able to drive nails into the framing's bottom plate, but drive some test nails to be sure.

You have two options. The first is to cut away a narrow strip of drywall or plaster near the top of the wainscoting, and replace it with a plywood nailer for attaching the tongue-and-groove boards.

The second option is to apply construction adhesive to the back of each board. Drive nails into the drywall or plaster to hold the boards in place while the adhesive dries.

STEP-BY-STEP >>> Finishing at the Top and Bottom

❶ **Cut a number of pieces** to the same length. When figuring the height of the wainscoting, take into account the width of the top cap. A simple jig, like this stop attached to a miter gauge on a table saw, makes it easy to mass-produce cuts.

❷ **It's important to install wainscoting plumb** and tight to the wall. Hold the first piece against the wall and use a level to see if you need to cut it.

Wainscoting

(Continued from previous page)

❸ If the wall isn't flat or plumb, tack your first piece in place against the wall so it is plumb, with the tongue side facing out. Set a compass slightly wider than the widest gap, and hold it against the wall as you trace a line along the board; this is called scribing. Remove the piece and cut along the line with a jigsaw.

❹ Reinstall with the untrimmed edge plumb and the trimmed edge against the wall. Check for plumb, then drive nails to attach.

❺ Attach a straight board to act as a temporary guide for the tops of the boards. Or, if you will not install base molding, be careful to butt the boards together at the floor so they form a straight line; the top trim can cover any imperfections in the top edge. Leave a ¹⁄₁₆-inch gap between the first and second boards to allow for expansion.

❻ At inside corners, butt the pieces together, with the tongue facing out. If the wall is not plumb, you will need to scribe and cut the affected board as shown in steps 2 and 3.

⑦ **At an outside corner, tack the first piece in place** and run a pencil along the back edge to mark for cutting it. Cut, then install the other piece in the same way, so it covers the edge of the board on the first wall.

⑧ **Remove the guide strip.** Cut nosing or panel trim to fit. (Cut pieces at 45-degree miters where they meet at an inside or outside corner.) Nail the top molding and the baseboard (if any) in place.

⑨ **Check for any gaps, and drive nails** to snug the top molding to the wall. Finish your new wainscoting with stain and sealer, or prime and paint.

TIP: NAILING TONGUE-AND-GROOVE WAINSCOTING

If the boards are thick and sturdy enough, you can angle-drive nails through the point where the tongue meets the main board; this will leave you with no visible nail holes. However, much wainscoting is too thin and fragile to be installed this way, so it is best to face-nail the boards, then fill the holes with wood putty later.

CHAPTER 2

When shopping for flooring, it's easy to become overwhelmed by the variety of products and range of prices. Some consumers are more confident in their selection if they actually buy several square feet of flooring, take it home, and see if it really fits their goals. Such persistence will be rewarded with the long-term satisfaction of floors that fit your style, needs, and budget.

Tile, once common only in a kitchen or bath, is now often installed in just about any room of the house. Ceramic tile may have a shiny glaze or a matte surface. Stone tiles may be smooth and glossy (granite and marble are the most common choices), or they can be rough and even irregular in shape. Choose tiles that will be durable and easy to maintain. Tiles made for walls are a poor choice for floors, where they're likely to crack.

Ceramic and stone tile must be installed onto a rock-solid subsurface, often made of plywood and concrete backerboard. Resilient flooring can flex, so the prep work is often easier. Carpet tiles are now available in many styles and colors, and can be either glued down or simply laid in place.

Refurbishing hardwood floors will enhance the look and the value of your home, but it's a big job that includes days of dust. If your floors are worn or stained, replacing them may be the better option. Hardwood planking is beyond our budget for any significant area, but consider wood parquet or "floating" strip flooring, which may have a natural wood or plastic laminate finish. These install quickly and easily.

Enhancing Floors

Flooring Preparation

For any type of flooring, the subsurface must be basically level, with no major dips or high spots. However, different types of flooring demand different subsurface preparation:

• For ceramic or stone tiles, the surface must be very firm so the tiles don't crack. Marble is extremely brittle and so demands a rock-solid subsurface. When an adult jumps on the floor, you should feel virtually no flexing. However, the floor does not have to be perfectly smooth; you can level out small imperfections when you trowel the mortar.

• For resilient tiles, the subsurface does not have to be flex-free, but it does need to be very smooth; most indentations and high spots will telegraph through the tiles and be very visible. Carpet tiles will show almost as many underlying imperfections.

• Floating floors do not need a very firm or a very smooth surface, and so are the easiest to prepare for.

New flooring will add value to your home only if the installation has a professional appearance. Careful and correct subsurface prep will make the new floor smooth, even, and durable.

MATERIALS & TOOLS:

• Flooring scraper, hammer, chisel, and other tools for removing old flooring
• Plywood or cement backerboard
• Thinset mortar or self-leveling compound
• Trowel
• Drill and screws
• Long level or straightedge board
• Hand or power sander
• Knife or backerboard cutter
• Circular saw and saber saw

Removing Old Flooring

To remove sheet flooring, slice through the sheet to make 15-inch-wide strips. Starting at a cut line, pry up the sheet with a flooring scraper, rolling the strip as you go. Use the same tool to remove resilient tile. If you also need to remove the plywood under the flooring, adjust a circular saw to cut just through the flooring and the plywood. Cut into manageable sections, and pry up the plywood and flooring all at once.

To remove existing ceramic tile, use a hammer or hand sledge and a cold chisel. Crack the tile with the hammer and use the chisel to pry up the tile.

Leveling

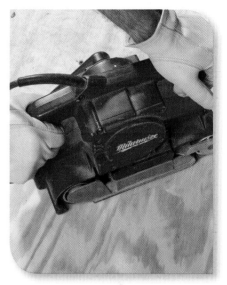

Use a knife to cut old carpet and pad into strips. Pull up a corner of the carpet with pliers, then your hands, and roll the strips up as you remove them. Remove any tack strips with a pry bar.

Lay a long level or other straightedge on the floor and move it around to find low and high spots. To fill a depression, mix and spread thinset mortar or floor leveling compound and use the trowel to feather the edges. When the mortar is dry, check with the straightedge, and sand as needed.

Where there is a high spot, drive screws into the supporting joists. If that doesn't work, use a belt sander or hand sander to level the area. If you plan to install resilient flooring or carpet tiles, check with a straightedge and your hand to be sure the surface is smooth.

Installing Underlayment

Laying Out the Job

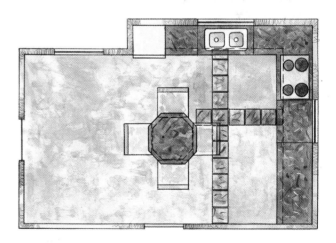

If the subfloor has deteriorated or if you need to add strength, install new underlayment; ¾-inch plywood is the usual choice. You may need to tear up the old underlayment to keep the new floor close to the level of adjacent flooring. Start with a full sheet squared to a corner. Center the plywood edge on the joist and drive screws into the joists. If you will be installing ceramic tile, install cement backerboard atop the plywood, as shown on page 41.

Take time to carefully lay out the job so you don't end up with highly visible rows of very narrow tiles or tiles that are obviously out of parallel with the adjoining wall. Make a detailed drawing of the room, showing all obstructions. Then plan where all the tiles will go. If you are installing ceramic tile, be sure to take into account the width of the grout lines. Wherever possible, plan to install tiles that are at least half-width along each wall.

Ceramic Tile

A well-laid ceramic tile floor imbues a room with elegance. And tile is especially cost-effective in small, high-visibilty areas, such as entryways and powder rooms—spaces well-suited to getting maximum value from a modest budget. The high traffic in such areas plays to the strength of tile, which can remain durable and easy to clean for decades.

Fortunately, you don't have to be a professional to get great results. Start with a solid and level backerboard surface, then use the tools and techniques described here to lay tiles consistently.

MATERIALS & TOOLS:

- Cement backerboard and backerboard screws
- Thinset mortar
- Fiberglass mesh tape
- Ceramic tiles and sanded grout
- Drill with hole-saw bits and screwdriver tips
- Backerboard cutter and knife
- Notched trowel
- Plastic spacers
- Snap cutter, tile nippers, and rental wet saw, if needed
- Grout float, sponge, and bucket
- Knee pads
- Caulk
- Level or other straightedge
- Tape measure and chalk line
- Carpet scrap and 2x4 to make a beater block

Substrates for Ceramic

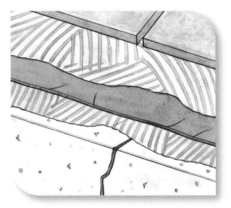

As long as the joists below are firm, this arrangement produces a strong-enough substrate. Start with ¾-inch plywood attached to the joists. (Existing hardwood flooring of the same thickness is just as strong, as long as it is in good shape.) On top of that, set ½-inch cement backerboard in a thinset mortar bed. Then you can trowel on thinset and install the tiles.

If you have a concrete slab in sound condition, apply a waterproofing membrane over it. This may be a liquid product that you trowel or roll on, or it may be a sheet that you set in a layer of thinset mortar. Allow to dry, and then you can set the tiles in thinset.

If a floor has large uneven areas, mix and pour on self-leveling compound. You may need to lightly smooth it, but it generally levels itself, as advertised. Quick-setting brands allow you to tile within hours.

STEP-BY-STEP >>>Backerboard

❶ Look for fastener lines on the floor to find the joists below, so you can drive some of the screws into the joists. Use a carbide backerboard cutter and a metal straightedge to cut through the board just enough to slice through the mesh beneath the surface.

❷ Hold both sides of the cut with your hands, and bump the scored line with your knee to snap it into a V shape. Use a knife to cut through the mesh on the other side until the pieces separate.

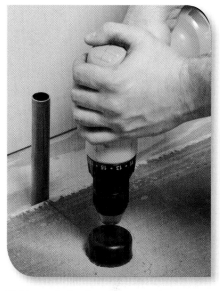

❸ To cut holes for pipes, set the backerboard edge against the pipe and mark the center of the hole. Cut with a hole saw. For larger holes, score with a knife, tap with a hammer, then score the other side with a knife and clear out the waste material from the hole.

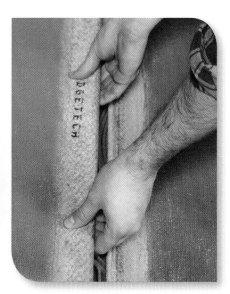

❹ Follow the manufacturer's directions to mix thinset mortar in a bucket. Spread the mortar using a square-notched trowel. First press the mortar with the flat side of the trowel, then comb with the notched side, holding the trowel at a consistent 45-degree angle for an even surface. Lower the backerboard onto the mortar.

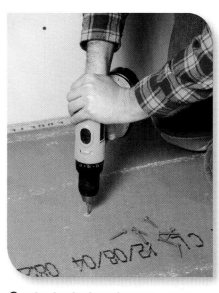

❺ Drive backerboard screws every 8 inches or so. Use 2-inch screws at the joists and 1¼-inch screws in the field. Drive the screwheads flush. As you lay succeeding sheets, leave a ⅛-inch gap between sheets and a ¼-inch gap at the walls.

❻ Press fiberglass tape over the joints, then apply a thin coat of thinset over the tape with a trowel. Feather the edges to eliminate any high spots.

Ceramic Tile

(Continued from previous page)

STEP-BY-STEP >>> Lay Out

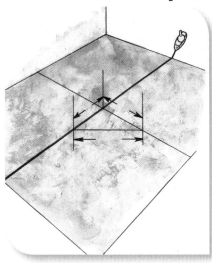

❶ Start with two perpendicular lines in the middle. To make sure the lines are square, lay two factory edges of a sheet of plywood (or backerboard or drywall) against them. Or mark 3 feet from the center along one leg and 4 feet on the other. If the diagonal distance between the marks is 5 feet, the lines are square.

❷ Dry-lay tiles in both directions along the lines, using the plastic spacers between them, and make sure you will end up with the desired size of tiles at the walls. You may then choose to adjust the layout.

❸ Once you have determined the layout, measure over from the original lines and snap parallel layout lines indicating the edges of the tiles in both directions.

STEP-BY-STEP >>> Setting Tiles

❶ Mix mortar in a bucket to the consistency of mayonnaise so it is wet but dry enough for the trowel ridges to hold their shape. Pour enough mortar to cover a section about 3 feet square. Spread with the flat side of a square-notched trowel, then comb with the notched side. Hold the trowel at a consistent 45-degree angle, and do not cover layout lines.

❷ Set the first tile at the intersection of the layout lines. Press gently and twist slightly to help embed it in the mortar. Keep the edges of the tile on the layout lines.

❸ Lay the next tile on the layout line in the same way. Set spacers upright between the tiles and snug the tiles against the spacers. Take care not to move the first tile as you do so.

④ After laying several tiles and before the mortar starts to stiffen, set a carpenter's level or other straightedge against the tile edges to make sure the tiles are lined up precisely. Adjust the tiles if needed.

⑤ Continue laying tiles and setting spacers, filling in the quadrant between the layout lines. At each corner, turn the upright spacers flat-side down and snug the corners of the tiles against the spacers.

TIPS: TILING

- Every few tiles, pick one up and examine the back; if less than 75 percent is covered with mortar, you may need to lay the mortar more thickly, press more firmly, or back-butter the tiles.

- Never step directly on tiles until the mortar is hardened. If you need to adjust a tile that is too far away to reach without stepping on other newly set tiles, place a piece of ¾-inch plywood, at least 2 feet square, over the tiles and step on that.

⑥ When you have completed one section, check with a level or other straightedge for tiles that are higher or lower than the rest of the surface. Tack a scrap piece of carpet to a 12- to 15-inch 2x4 to make a beater block. Tap high tiles in place using the beater block and a hammer or rubber mallet.

⑦ If a tile is lower than others, pry it up with a knife or screwdriver and back-butter it—spread more thinset on its back. Reset the tile and level it with the beater block. Clean excess mortar out of joints by dragging a spacer along the joint. Allow the mortar to cure overnight.

Making Curved Cuts

To cut out a curve, use a wet saw to make a series of closely spaced cuts that reach just to the cut line. Clamp the jaws of tile nippers about an inch away from the line and snap out the waste. Then hold the nippers along the cut line, squeeze tightly, and pry off the remaining waste. Nip off just a little at a time.

Ceramic Tile

(Continued from previous page)

Cutting Tiles

On a large job you may choose to install only the full-sized tiles on the first day, then install the cut tiles on the next day; this may save you a day's rental for a wet saw. If you've never cut tiles before, make some practice cuts until you are satisfied with your skills.

Tiles are rarely cut to fit snugly; it is best to leave a gap between tiles and walls, pipes, or other obstructions that is about the same as your grout width. Depending on the baseboard molding or shoe that you will install after tiling, you may have ¾-inch leeway.

To mark for a straight cut, set the tile to be cut directly on top of an installed tile. Place a marker tile over the tile to be cut, with its edge against the wall. Mark the edge with a pencil or marker, then mark the actual cut line parallel to the edge but shorter by the width of two grout lines.

To make an L-shaped cut at an outside corner, set the tile to be cut first on one side of the corner, then the other, marking the cut lines with a full tile as you would for a straight cut. Then mark each side shorter than the mark by the width of two grout lines.

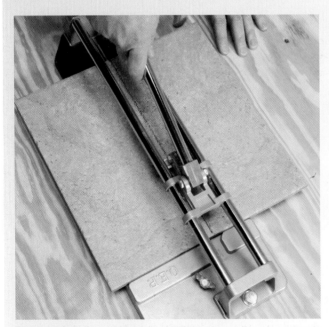

Use a simple snap cutter for straight cuts. Align the cutter's scoring wheel with the cut line. Press down and pull or push the cutter to score a single line in one pass. Raise and press down on the handle to snap the tile along the cut line.

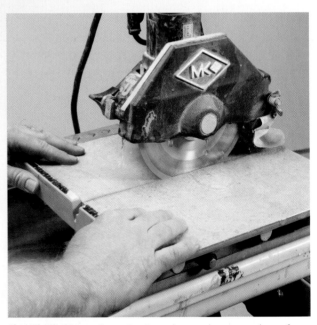

If you need to make cutouts or have a large number of cuts, rent a wet saw. Be sure to keep water spraying onto the blade at all times; even a few seconds of dry cutting can dull the blade. Align the tile's cut line with the blade, and gently push the tile through to make the cut.

STEP-BY-STEP >>> Grouting

❶ Allow the mortar to harden, at least overnight and longer if humidity is high. Pry out all the spacers. Scrape or slice out any mortar that is within ¼ inch of the tile surface.

❷ Mix a batch of latex-reinforced, sanded grout to the consistency of toothpaste. Pour a dollop onto the floor and spread with a laminated grout float. First hold the float nearly flat and press the grout into the joints. Then tilt the float up to scrape away excess.

❸ Work the float diagonally to the joints to avoid digging into the spaces. Use long, sweeping strokes to remove about 80 percent of the excess grout.

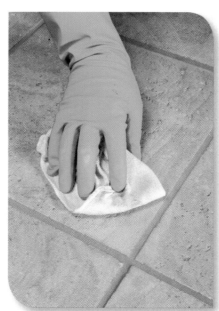

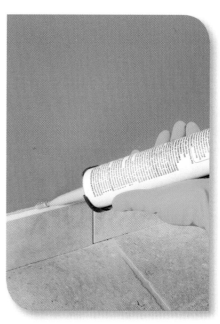

❹ Dampen a large sponge and wipe the surface gently, taking care not to dig into the grout lines. Use a circular motion. Continually rinse the sponge in clean water, and change the water frequently.

❺ Sponge several times, and work to produce grout lines that are consistent in depth and width. Allow to dry, then wipe away the grout haze with a clean, dry cloth.

❻ Apply caulk to the joint between the tiles and the wall. Caulk is flexible, so it will prevent cracking due to expansion of the tiles. Add baseboards or base shoe as needed.

Mosaic Tile

Mosaic tiles come in sheets, most often with a mesh backing that holds all those little tiles neatly with perfect spacing. That means installing them will be easier than you may have thought.

The trick is to get the mortar just the right consistency—not too wet and not too dry—and just the right height, so all of the tiles are embedded in mortar, but the mortar does not squeeze out between them. Epoxy-reinforced mortar is worth the extra cost because it grabs the tiles firmly. Be sure to consult with your dealer or the manufacturer's instructions to get a trowel with notches of the correct size.

Install a strong subsurface, ideally with cement backerboard, as shown on pages 40–41. A floor that flexes will not cause individual mosaic tiles to crack, but it will create cracks in the grout.

Before you mix the mortar, dry-lay a number of mosaic sheets. If a wall is out of square, it could cause a noticeably angled line; you may be able to adjust the layout so that the most noticeable wall has tiles that run parallel to it. If you will be installing a pattern with two or more types of mosaic sheets, cut and lay out all the sheets before you start.

Mosaic floor tiles are a classic and still-popular look for a bathroom and perhaps a small entryway. If you are new to tiling, avoid complicated tile patterns that increase the challenge. Be sure the subsurface is smooth and even; any waves will be noticeable in the final tiled surface.

MATERIALS & TOOLS:
- Sheets of mosaic tiles
- Epoxy- or latex-reinforced thinset mortar
- Reinforced grout
- Utility knife
- Notched trowel
- Snap cutter and tile nippers or wet saw
- Beater board and mallet
- Level or other straightedge
- Grout float and large sponge
- Chalk lines

STEP-BY-STEP >>>

❶ **Snap layout lines and mix** and apply mortar as shown on page 42. Take care not to cover the layout lines with the mortar. Carefully place the first sheet aligned with the two layout lines so you do not have to slide it more than ½ inch or so. Lay subsequent sheets in the same way. Make sure the tiles of abutting sheets are spaced the same as tiles within a sheet. Press lightly, then use a beater board and mallet to embed the tiles.

❷ **Every so often, pull up a sheet** to check for full coverage. All tiles must be stuck in mortar. If not, pull up the sheet and add and comb more mortar onto the floor; don't try to back-butter a mosaic sheet. You may find that you need to push down more lightly with the notched trowel as you comb, so the mortar is a bit higher.

❸ Use a straightedge to keep the layout straight as you continue to lay sheets. Take special care to wipe away any squeezed-up mortar with a slightly damp sponge.

❹ You can remove individual tiles by cutting the sheet's mesh with a utility knife. Cutting individual tiles may be a bit tricky. If the tile is large enough, you can use a snap cutter. For very small pieces like this, use tile nippers or a wet saw. Back-butter cut tiles with mortar before setting them.

❺ Allow the mortar to harden, at least overnight and longer if the air is humid. Mix grout in a bucket to the consistency of mayonnaise. Pour a dollop on the floor, and use a grout float, held nearly flat, to push the grout into all the joints. Move the float in several directions at all points to make sure every space is

filled. Tilt the float up at a steep angle and use it like a squeegee to wipe away most of the excess grout. Move the float diagonally to the joints to avoid digging into them.

❻ Use a damp—not wet—sponge to remove excess grout. Press very lightly as you work, and use a circular motion so you maintain grout lines that are just slightly recessed. Rinse the sponge often and change the water in the bucket frequently. Wipe two or three times. Allow to dry, then buff with a clean, dry cloth.

Stone Tile

Rough stone tiles, most commonly made of split-cut slate, are not perfectly formed like ceramic tile or granite or marble tiles. Usually (though not always) they are consistent in width and length, but often they vary quite a bit in thickness. That means you may need to spend some extra time back-buttering the thinner pieces, and perhaps picking up and scraping away mortar from thicker pieces, in order to achieve a smooth finished surface. A bit of imperfection is expected with a rough-stone floor, but it's still a good idea to aim for near-perfection.

Stone tile (except granite) is easily cracked so follow the steps on pages 40–41 to make a firm, inflexible substrate. Lay the tiles in a dry run, adjust their positions for the best overall look, and snap chalk lines to lay out the job out as you would for ceramic tile (pages 42–43).

Slate tiles like the ones shown here are relatively inexpensive, yet they can produce a richly textured and multicolored floor. Because these tiles vary greatly in color and texture, buy more than you need and take time to sort through them and eliminate any unattractive ones. Then arrange the different colors on the floor to get the precise "random order" that appeals to you.

MATERIALS & TOOLS:

- Stone tiles
- Plastic spacers
- Reinforced thinset mortar
- Reinforced grout
- Masonry sealer and paint brush
- Square-notched trowel
- Wet saw or grinder with masonry blade
- Grout float and large sponge
- Beater board and mallet

STEP-BY-STEP >>>

❶ **Stone tiles often have a layer of dust.** To ensure good adhesion, wipe the dust away with a wet sponge. Let the tiles dry before laying them.

❷ **Because rough stone tiles are porous,** grout can seep into them while you are grouting, creating a "grout haze" that can be difficult to clean away. To prevent this, coat the tops of the tiles with a masonry sealer. Take care to coat the tops only—not the sides, where you want grout to stick.

❸ Trowel thinset onto the floor with a square-notched trowel, taking care not to cover the layout lines. Back-butter most or all of the tiles to ensure sticking. Add more mortar to the backs of thinner tiles (or to thinner portions of tiles, which may be irregular in thickness). Set the tiles in the thinset and use plastic spacers to maintain even grout lines. Tap with a beater board to set the tiles and make a smooth surface. You may sometimes need to lift a tile and add or remove mortar.

❹ Install all the full-size tiles, and wipe away mortar from around the edges. Cut the edge tiles with a wet saw. If several tiles need to be cut at the same width, use the saw's guide to mass-cut them. Back-butter and lay the tiles, taking care to set them at the same height as the adjacent tiles.

❺ Let the edge tiles cure for 24 hours. Mix a batch of sanded reinforced grout. Wipe the edges of the tiles with a damp sponge to moisten them. Apply grout as shown on page 45. Once the grout has cured, apply sealer to the entire surface.

TIP: GRINDER CUTTING

If you have only a few cuts to make, you can achieve fairly neat results using a grinder equipped with a masonry cutting blade. After cutting a cutout like the one shown, snap the waste out with your hands, then use nippers to clean up the corner. If you have a lot of cuts to make, spend more for a diamond blade.

Resilient Tile

Dry-back resilient tile, also known as vinyl composition or commercial tile, comes in a variety of colors and has flecks of color that effectively hide dirt. Most types have a subtle grain that faces in a direction indicated by arrows on the back of the tile, so you can give the floor a distinctive look by laying them with the arrows facing in alternating directions. Or install them all with arrows facing the same way for a more seamless look.

Colors may vary. Talk with your dealer to be sure all of your tiles come from the same dye lot. If that's not possible, spend some time shuffling the tiles in a dry run on the floor, to achieve a pleasingly random effect.

The subsurface does not have to be strong or firm, but it does need to be very smooth; even minor subsurface imperfections will appear on the finished floor within a year. Take time to fill any low spots, sink and fill nails or screws, and sand the surface smooth before installing the tile. Remove the baseboard's shoe molding or the baseboard itself, as well as any other obstructions.

These tiles are inexpensive, don't require strengthening of the floor, and barely raise the level of the floor, making them a very practical solution in many cases. They are associated in many people's minds with grocery stores and school hallways. But "commercial" tile can have a lively look if installed in colorful patterns, most commonly checkerboards.

If you choose colors that harmonize nicely with the room's décor, you can achieve a warm, inviting, playful look for a very modest cost. These tiles are certainly suitable for a basement or a playroom, and can also look great in a kitchen.

MATERIALS & TOOLS:
- Resilient tiles
- Resilient tile adhesive
- Small-notched trowel
- Utility knife and straightedge
- Pencil and tape measure
- Vinyl flooring roller (rented from a flooring supply store)
- Chalk line

STEP-BY-STEP >>>

❶ **Provide a smooth subsurface,** and snap layout chalk lines as shown on page 42. Starting at the intersection of the lines, spread resilient tile adhesive with the flat side of a small-notched trowel (check the adhesive can for the correct notch size). Then comb the adhesive with the notched side. Let the adhesive set until it's tacky.

❷ **Carefully lower the first tile** onto the floor, perfectly aligned with the layout lines. Do not press down yet. Check the grain direction, and lay the second piece with its edge pressed against the first tile. Once you have laid four or five tiles, press down on the tiles; they will not slide after that.

❸ **To mark edge tiles for cutting,** set a loose tile exactly on top of the tile closest to the wall. Set a marker tile on top of that one, positioned against ¼-inch spacers placed against the wall. Check that the grain is facing the correct way. Run a pencil along the edge of the marker tile to mark the cut.

❹ **Place a straightedge along the cut** line, and score the surface with a utility knife. Make several passes until you cut most of the way through, then snap the tile with your hands. If the cut end will be visible, keep scoring until you cut all the way through.

❺ **Clean off any squeezed-out adhesive** using mineral spirits, water and detergent, or a solvent recommended by the manufacturer. Run a flooring roller over the entire floor. Reinstall the baseboard's shoe or the baseboard.

Self-Stick Vinyl Tiles

Peel-and-stick tiles are typically thinner than dry-backed resilient tile, so they show underlying imperfections even more clearly. Take special care to make the subsurface very smooth. Many claim that you can simply peel off the paper backing and press them into place, but pros always apply at least a sealer, and often resilient flooring adhesive, to ensure long-lasting adhesion.

Dry-lay the tiles, then snap layout lines. Apply the recommended primer or resilient flooring adhesive, and allow to dry. You may need to apply two coats of primer. Peel off the paper backing and gently lay several tiles in place, against the layout lines and tight against each other. Once the tiles are stuck to the floor, they cannot be moved without cracking them. To cut the tiles, you can use a knife or a pair of scissors.

Parquet Tile

Parquet tiles are made of many small wood strips to create a richly textured appearance. Installation requires a floor that is basically even, but the subsurface does not have to be very smooth or very strong.

Parquet tiles vary greatly in price—and in quality. Examine some samples before you make a purchase. Inexpensive tiles may have tongue-and-groove edges that do not fit together snugly, bonding glue that does not hold the strips together well, and less-than-durable finishes. Those problems can make installation difficult and may mean that you need to apply a polyurethane finish on top, but may not affect the finished floor's performance. Be aware that parquet adhesive is expensive, and may be a major part of the materials expense.

Quality, color, and proper installation make all the difference. If you choose richly colored tiles that are free of imperfections, install them nestled tightly together, and keep the floor well sealed, then the finished product will make a room feel warm and stately. Dry-lay a number of tiles to be sure they will harmonize with other colors in the room. Dark oak and cherry colors have a more substantial feel than lighter tiles that resemble maple or pine. Parquet tiles are suitable for most any room other than a bathroom, and they're ideal for public areas such as entryways.

MATERIALS & TOOLS:

- Wood parquet tiles
- Parquet tile adhesive
- Notched trowel
- Circular saw or other power saw
- Tape measure and chalk line

Parquet tiles are most commonly installed in a diamond pattern, but dry-lay some tiles on the floor to see if you might prefer a herringbone or pyramid pattern instead.

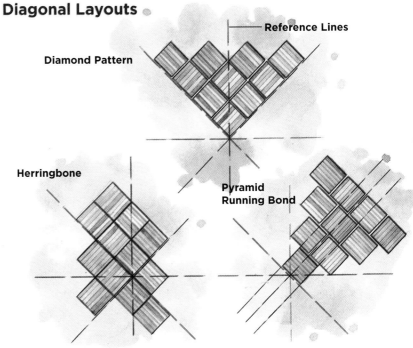

Diagonal Layouts

Reference Lines

Diamond Pattern

Herringbone

Pyramid
Running Bond

STEP-BY-STEP >>>

❶ Lay tiles in a dry run to help determine layout. Snap layout chalk lines as shown on page 42. Using a trowel with notches of the recommended size, spread parquet flooring adhesive. Set the first tile with its edges against the two layout lines. Use the edge of the tile—not the tongue—to line up the tile. Avoid sliding the tiles more than a half inch or so, or you may push adhesive into the grooves.

❷ Insert the tongue of the next tile into the groove of the first, then press it gently down and into place. You can usually adjust tile positions for about 15 minutes, until the adhesive sets up.

❸ Continue installing tiles in the same way. Cut tiles using a circular saw or other power saw. Leave a space of ¼ inch between tiles and the wall, to allow for expansion due to humidity; if you don't do this, the floor may buckle.

TIP: SETTING ON THE DIAGONAL

To set tiles on a diagonal, strike layout lines that are 45 degrees to the walls and 90 degrees to one another. You will need to cut many perimeter pieces at 45 degrees.

Cork Tiles

Natural cork flooring is easy on the feet as well as the eyes, making it a happy choice for kitchens and other areas where people stand for long periods. Cork is available as planks that are set in floating fashion, as shown on pages 58–61. But you can also install cork as tiles, which are available in natural tones or in a variety of colors. Be sure to use adhesive made specifically for cork tiles; all-purpose and other types of adhesive won't hold.

The subfloor should be very smooth, but it does not have to be extra firm. Snap layout lines as shown on page 42. Spread the adhesive using a trowel with notches of the

recommended size, and allow it to become tacky. Set the first tile against two intersecting layout lines, but do not press down. Lay several more tiles and make sure they are aligned with the layout lines before pressing down. Clean away any squeezed-up adhesive immediately using a recommended solvent or detergent. Cut tiles with a knife and straightedge.

Once all the tiles are laid, run a flooring roller over the floor. Seal the entire floor with a urethane product recommended by the manufacturer. Keep the floor well sealed; moisture can damage it.

Carpet Tile

At a home center or from online sources you can find a wide array of carpet tiles in various colors, piles, and thicknesses. Some types are installed using mastic, but most carpet tiles today come with a self-stick adhesive that is exposed when a backing paper is removed. Some types are heavy enough that they require only a slightly sticky backing to stay in place.

Thinner carpet tiles will show minor underlying imperfections, but thicker tiles will cover up some hidden sins. In any event, it will be easy to remove and reinstall a tile if you need to smooth out the surface below. Before you start, remove the room's base shoe or baseboard molding.

This can be a quick way to transform a room. Bright and contrasting colors can be used in a child's bedroom, a basement, or a playroom. In living areas you can use carpet tiles to provide a neutral background with a bit more interest than plain carpeting.

MATERIALS & TOOLS:

- Carpet tiles
- Tape measure and chalk line
- Utility knife and straightedge

STEP-BY-STEP >>>

❶ **Measure and chalk layout lines** as shown on page 42. Dry-lay a number of tiles until you are certain of the layout, then remove the paper backing and install the first tile aligned with the layout lines.

❷ **As you lay succeeding tiles,** pay attention to the arrows on the sticky side. Install tiles all facing the same direction, or use an alternating pattern.

❸ **After installing all the full-size tiles,** use a straightedge and a utility knife to cut the perimeter tiles. Be sure to keep them facing in the correct direction. It may take several passes to cut through the tile. Once all the tiles are laid, run a flooring roller over the surface and reinstall the base shoe.

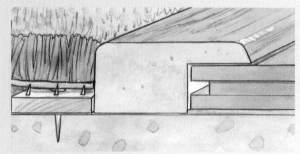

Floor Transitions

Where one floor surface meets another in a doorway, choose a transition or threshold that complements both types of flooring and that makes a graceful shift from one to the other. The steps below show cutting and installing a metal transition. The illustrations below show some of the most common alternatives. Transitions are typically made of metal, wood, or natural stone.

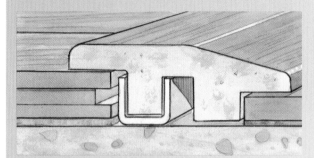

A reducer strip makes the move from a lower to a higher floor less noticeable.

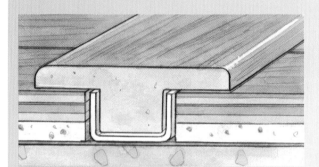

T-molding transitions between two floors of the same height.

When wood flooring butts against carpeting, a universal threshold is often the most attractive option.

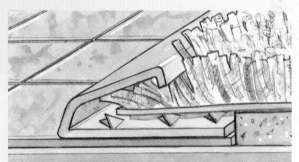

Carpet edging has a tack strip that holds the carpet in place. After the carpet is installed, the lip is folded down to clasp the carpet.

STEP-BY-STEP >>>

❶ **Measure the width of the doorway** and subtract ¹⁄₁₆ inch so the transition will fit easily. You may be able to slide the transition under a door's molding, or you may need to cut it at an angle to make it fit snugly.

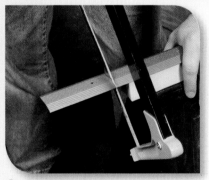

❷ **Mark the transition for cutting.** In some cases it is best to cut both sides so as to end up with nail holes fairly close to each end. Clamp a metal transition and cut with a hacksaw or tin snips. Use a miter saw to cut a wood transition.

❸ **Position the transition** and make sure it covers the edges of both floorings. Drive nails or screws to fasten the transition securely.

Base Molding

Base molding gets bumped by the vacuum cleaner and may get scratched by pets or children's toys. And in an older home many repaintings may give it an unattractive alligator-skin appearance. You can try filling in holes with wood putty and sanding, but the results will never be as clean-looking as what you can achieve by replacing it.

To remove old molding, use a utility knife to cut through the paint where the molding meets the wall. Place a taping blade against the wall to protect it, and pry the molding out with a flat pry bar. If the new molding is not as wide as the old, you may need to sand and patch the newly exposed wall.

Base molding is available in a variety of styles, the most popular being ranch and colonial. Most often, a base shoe is added to the bottom.

Beat-up baseboard moldings really do make a room feel shabby, and replacing them with crisp-lined moldings will subtly but effectively brighten the ambience. Choose moldings that harmonize with the others in the room. Painted pine is generally the least expensive option and the safest choice for a do-it-yourselfer. But if you are confident of your skills, you may choose to really spruce things up by replacing all the moldings—including the window and door casings—with stained hardwood.

MATERIALS & TOOLS:
- Base molding and perhaps base shoe
- Finishing nails
- Hammer and nail set or power nailer
- Drill
- Power miter saw or hand miter box
- Framing square
- T-bevel

TIP: LAY OUT THE JOB

Mark the walls lightly to indicate stud locations so you can attach the molding to framing. Cope cut an inside corner, as described *opposite*, coping the pieces that are least visible from the doorway.

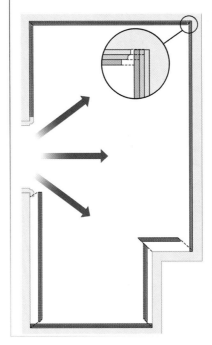

Built-Up Base Moldings

The most common arrangement is a single piece of base molding coupled with a base shoe, but there are many other options. The combinations pictured below show how different looks can be achieved from simple stock pieces.

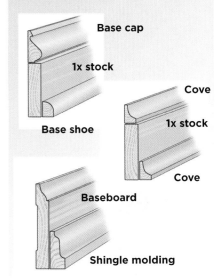

Base cap
1x stock
Base shoe
Cove
1x stock
Cove
Baseboard
Shingle molding

STEP-BY-STEP >>>

❶ Outside corners are often out of square. Use a framing square to check. If the corner is a perfect 90 degrees, you can simply cut the pieces at 45-degree bevels.

❷ If the corner is out of square, use a scrap piece of wood to draw lines on the floor parallel to each wall.

❸ Set a T-bevel to run from the wall corner to the intersection of the lines.

❹ Set the saw to cut at the angle you captured with the T-bevel, and cut one piece at that bevel. Set the angle to the other side to cut the second baseboard.

❺ Check each piece for a snug but not over-tight fit, then attach to the wall with finish nails driven into the baseplate and the studs. Install all the baseboard pieces, then install base shoe, if desired. Use coped joints, as shown below, at inside corners.

Coped Joint for an Inside Corner

At an inside corner you could simply miter the joint, cutting each piece at a 45-degree bevel. But the result is often a less-than-tight joint. A coped joint is much more reliable and workmanlike. Start by installing the first piece on the wall cut at a simple 90 degrees.

❶ Cut the next piece at a 45-degree bevel, with the back of the molding longer than the face. Use a hand saw to cut along the straight section, following the line on the face of the board made by the miter cut. Angle the cut slightly back so that the front of the molding is slightly longer than the back.

❷ Use a coping saw to cut the angled portions. Back cut so that only a thin edge will make contact at the joint. Use a knife to pare away any high spots.

❸ Push the coped piece against the already installed piece on the wall. Measure and cut the other end as needed. Attach with nails driven into the wall plate and studs. Install a base shoe in the same way.

Snap-Together Floating Floor

A "floating" floor is made of planks that are not attached to the surface below. Instead, they rest on top of foam underlayment. This makes it not only easy to install but also gentler on the feet. Installing a floating floor can be a quick and fairly inexpensive way to rejuvenate a room.

Some types of floating floor are glued together at the seams, requiring a series of shims and clamps to hold the planks together while the glue dries. These pages show an easier installation, using planks that snap (or "click") together, so that no glue is needed.

Floating snap-together flooring is available as engineered flooring, which has a veneer of natural wood on top; or as laminate flooring, which has a hard plastic surface that has been convincingly printed to look like natural wood. Laminate flooring resists scratching better than engineered flooring, but once a scratch does occur, laminate flooring cannot be repaired whereas an engineered floor can be sanded and resealed.

The existing floor should be relatively even, with no visible waves. But it does not need to be very strong, and the flooring will span over small holes and indentations. If the floating floor will raise the floor level more than ½ inch above an adjacent floor (usually, at a doorway), you may choose to remove existing flooring to bring the level down.

MATERIALS & TOOLS:

- Engineered or laminate snap-together flooring
- Foam underlayment and recommended tape
- Shims
- Tape measure
- Hammer
- Tapping block or pull bar
- Circular saw or other power saw
- Utility knife
- Trim saw
- Flat pry bar and wide putty knife
- Combination square and pencil

TIP: SORT PLANKS

Leave the planks in the room for two days so they can acclimate to the humidity. Open the cartons and mix the planks so color variations are fairly evenly distributed throughout the room.

Getting Ready

If you plan to install over a concrete floor, start by laying down a moisture barrier of polyethylene sheeting, at least 6 mil thick. Tug to remove any wrinkles, and overlap the seams by 8 inches or more. Then roll the foam underlayment over the polyethylene.

STEP-BY-STEP >>>

❶ Remove the baseboard shoe, or the baseboard itself. Cut the line between the trim and the wall to prevent the paint from cracking. Use a wide putty knife to protect adjacent surfaces, and pry with a flat pry bar.

❷ Vacuum or sweep the floor clear of debris. Roll out the foam underlayment, and tug gently to remove any wrinkles. Cut the underlayment with a utility knife. Butt the sides of the pieces together; do not overlap them. Apply tape to the joints.

❸ Rip-cut the first planks if necessary. Along one wall, snap the first row of planks together with their tongues facing out. When you reach the end, measure and cut the last piece. If this piece is shorter than 6 inches, unsnap one plank. Center the remaining planks and cut longer pieces for each end.

❹ Cut the planks so they come ¼ inch short of the wall on each end. Use a combination square to draw a square line on the back side. Cut with a circular saw or any other power saw.

❺ Snap the first row of planks together end to end. Push them against the wall, then insert ¼-inch spacers every foot or so. This space will allow the planks to expand during changes in humidity; planks pressed tight against the wall may buckle.

❻ Install the next row of planks in the same way. However, you must offset the planks by at least 3 inches or as directed by the manufacturer. This means that your cuts on the second row will be different from those on the first row. To snap planks side by side, tilt the second plank and push its groove onto the tongue of the first plank. Lower the plank until it snaps into place.

Undercut Door Trim

Don't try to notch the flooring to go around door trim. Instead, set a plank next to the trim and cut the bottom of the trim with a saw. You can use a regular handsaw, but a special door trim saw like the one shown is easier and neater.

Snap-Together Floating Floor

(Continued from previous page)

TIP: TIGHTENING UP

Check continually for gaps between the planks. It often helps to use a scrap block of wood and a hammer to close up gaps.

❼ Tilt and snap the next piece of the second row, then slide it over so it engages with the first piece. Or assemble all the pieces of the second row, then snap them into the first row.

❽ To help slide planks over so they snap end to end, it often helps to use a special pry bar, which may be supplied by the flooring manufacturer. Slip one end of the pry bar onto the end of the board, and tap on the other end until it snaps. The pry bar is especially useful for installing the last plank in a row.

TIP: AVOIDING A SLIVER

To make sure you don't end up with an unattractive narrow sliver along one wall, measure the width of the room. Divide the result by the width of the planks; the remainder equals the width of the final board you will install if you start with a full board. If the remainder is wide enough to be inconspicuous, go ahead and start with a full board. If not, add the remainder to the width of a plank and divide by 2. Rip-cut the first plank to this width; the last plank will be cut to the same width.

❾ Continue cutting and laying planks in the same way. Offset joints by at least 3 inches, and carefully watch for gaps that need to be tightened up.

❿ When you come to the last row, set shims against the wall and measure the width in several places. If the wall is very straight you may be able to cut all the planks to the same width, but more likely you will need to measure and cut each plank individually. Use a circular saw with a clamped straightedge, as shown, or use any other power saw.

⑪ **Tilt the final row and pull** as you lower it to snap it in place. Use a tapping block or a pull bar to tighten up this last row.

⑫ **Reinstall the base shoe** or baseboard. Drive nails into the wall, not into the flooring, which should be able to move slightly to accommodate changes in temperatures and humidity.

Scribing Along a Curved Wall

After snapping together two or three rows of planks, check for wide gaps along any waves in the wall. (Small gaps will be covered when you reinstall the base shoe or baseboard.) If you find a wide gap, use a compass to scribe a line on the planks to follow the contours of the wall. Disassemble the planks and use a jigsaw to cut along the scribed line. Reassemble and reinstall the planks with shims against the wall.

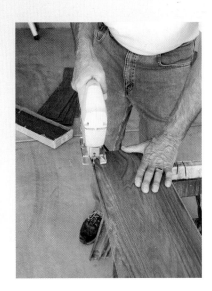

Painting a Floor

A painted wood floor has old-fashioned charm with a personal touch, and painting is often by far the easiest and least expensive way to spruce up a floor in poor condition.

Porch and deck enamel is usually the best paint choice, because it is strong and comes in a wide variety of colors. Oil- or alkyd-based paint is the most durable, but it may not be available in your area and you may not want to deal with the fumes. Water-based floor paint, especially 100 percent acrylic, is nearly as long lasting. If you cover the paint with a couple of coats of polyurethane, the surface will be even easier to keep clean and will resist scuffs and wear.

Here we show painting a wood floor with a single color. To paint a checkerboard pattern, see pages 64–65. Paining a concrete garage floor is a very different enterprise, described on pages 66–67.

MATERIALS & TOOLS:

- Hammer, pry bar, and taping blade
- Hand sander with sheets of 80-grit sandpaper
- Extension pole for sanding, cleaning, and rolling paint
- Vacuum cleaner
- Scrubber or mop and mild detergent
- Wood filler
- Floor paint, and perhaps polyurethane finish
- Paintbrush
- Paint roller with sleeve
- Paint tray
- Painter's masking tape

STEP-BY-STEP >>>

❶ Pry away the base shoe or baseboard, using a flat pry bar and a taping blade to protect nearby surfaces. Number the boards on their backs so you can reinstall them in the same order, or plan to install new base shoe. Alternatively, apply painter's tape to the base shoe, or, if you want to paint the shoe, to the base molding.

❷ Remove or hammer down any protruding nails. Fill large gaps with wood filler. Sand the surface with a hand sander equipped with a sheet of 80-grit sandpaper; pay special attention to any rough spots, and be sure to degloss any shiny surfaces.

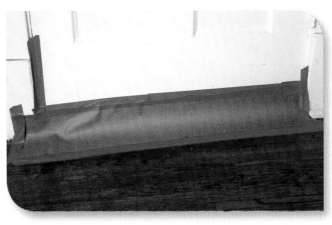

❸ **Vacuum the floor, then wash it with a mild detergent** solution (don't use oil-based soap). Look the floor over to determine if it is as smooth and consistent as you want. A painted floor is not expected to be perfect, but if you like the "shabby chic" look, be sure any roughness and gaps between boards will be consistent floor-wide.

❹ **Rinse the floor, and make sure it is dust free.** Even a small amount of dust on the wet paint will create a bumpy surface, so cover bottoms of doorways and shut windows while you work. You may choose to open one window and put a fan there, pointed outward.

❺ **Paint the perimeter of the floor with a brush.** Taping the brush to a pole will be a great relief to your back and knees.

❻ **Equip a paint roller with a medium-nap sleeve** and an extension pole. Roll paint as close to the edge as possible. Roll with the grain. If you see gaps between boards, roll again, this time against the grain. Finish by rolling lightly with the grain, and lifting the roller at the end of each stroke. Wherever possible, keep a wet edge.

TIP: FILLING GAPS

• If your floor has noticeable gaps between boards, make a design decision. If the gaps are consistently spread across the floor surface, and if you don't mind a rustic appearance, you may choose to leave them alone. However, the resulting floor will be a bit more difficult to keep clean.

• Don't expect paint to fill any but the slimmest of gaps. To fill anything wider, apply wood filler with a putty knife or taping blade. Allow to dry completely, then sand. You may need to repeat this process for wide gaps after the filler dries, because it will shrink a bit.

TIP: PAINTING VINYL FLOORING

Vinyl tiles or sheet flooring can be painted as long as it is firmly affixed to the floor at all points. First clean the vinyl thoroughly to remove any grease (which may not be visible). If there is mildew, clean with a solution of two parts water to one part household bleach. Sand the floor to roughen the glossy surface, and rinse thoroughly. Just before painting, wipe with a deglossing liquid so the paint will stick to the little holes in the vinyl where the sanding could not reach. Allow the deglossing liquid to dry, then paint.

Painting a Checkerboard Floor

C reating a checkerboard design on a floor takes more time and patience than simply painting one color, but it calls for no special skills. And the design options are endless. Light and pastel shades create a cottage look, while painting with deep contrasting colors can make a more formal appearance.

Start by prepping the floor and painting a base coat, as described on pages 62–63. Use a high-quality porch and deck enamel, and take special care to keep dust away while the paint dries. Inspect the paint job, and apply a second coat if needed; it will be difficult to add a second coat after you've painted the checkerboard. After the base coat's surface has dried, point a fan at it and allow the paint to dry and harden thoroughly; if possible, stay off the floor for a few days to be sure you do not mar the surface as you apply the checkerboard squares.

MATERIALS & TOOLS:

- Two colors of porch and deck enamel
- Painter's tape
- Tape measure and pencil
- Plastic or metal taping blade or putty knife
- Chalk line
- Paintbrush
- Paint roller and tray

STEP-BY-STEP >>>

❶ Measure the room and plan your checkerboard pattern. Here we show 12-inch squares, but you may prefer different sizes. Lay the job out so you don't end up with narrow slivers at a wall; you may choose to have, say, half-sized squares at either side. Use a tape measure and pencil to mark all four walls for the layout.

❷ Work with a helper to snap chalk lines between layout lines and create the checkerboard grid. To minimize chalk dust, pull the line out while holding it over a garbage can, then carry it to the floor. While your helper holds the line firmly on top of one layout line, pull it taut and place your end over the other line. Lift up and let go to make a perfectly straight line.

❸ To keep from getting confused, place a piece of tape inside each square that will not get painted. Apply pieces of tape with their inside edges against the perimeter of the squares that will get painted. To cut a piece of tape, firmly hold a putty knife nearly flat on top of it, and pull up on the tape. Some of these cuts must be made perfectly aligned to the layout lines.

❹ Rub the tape with the putty knife to make sure it is firmly stuck at all points. Do a thorough job to prevent paint from slipping under the tape.

❺ Paint the perimeter of the squares with a brush. Place the brush on the tape and wipe toward the square to reduce the risk of paint seeping under the tape. Brush-paint six or seven squares and then move on to the next step, so the perimeter paint does not have time to dry.

❻ Use a roller with a medium-nap sleeve to fill the squares. Don't overload the roller; give it just enough to cover the areas. Cover the brushed areas so the entire square will have the same texture.

❼ Soon after the paint has dried to the touch, pull the tape off the floor, lifting straight up or angling slightly toward the inside of the painted area. Throw the tape out immediately. If your hands get paint on them or if you make spills, wash them immediately. Once the floor has been painted, allow it to dry to the touch, then aim a fan at it and allow at least a day for it to dry.

TIP: A HALF-BARE PATTERN

If the existing floor is in good shape, you may choose to apply only one coat and leave half of the squares bare. Use the same technique for taping and painting as shown on these pages. In this example the squares were incompletely painted or partially wiped, for a distressed look.

Painting a Garage Floor

E poxy paint, often called "garage paint," is a huge upgrade from plain concrete. An epoxy finish, if correctly applied to a well-cleaned concrete surface, will repel oils and grime that would soak into bare concrete.

Here we show applying a two-part epoxy finish. You can also buy one-part garage floor paint, which is less expensive; just paint it on without any mixing. Many people report satisfactory results using the one-part paint, but the two-part method is more durable. Solvent-based epoxy is the strongest but may not be available or even legal in your area, and it produces noxious fumes when applied. Water-based two-part epoxy is nearly as durable, and is generally available at home centers and hardware stores. For extra protection, also apply a clear coat of sealer or whatever is recommended by the paint manufacturer.

As you'll notice from the steps on these pages, floor preparation is the key. If any oils are left on the floor, the paint may not stick to it, resulting in flaking and bare spots.

A clean-looking garage can be a definite selling point, and a quality paint job that promises to resist staining can transform an eyesore into something inviting.

MATERIALS & TOOLS:

- Degreasing solution
- Muriatic acid
- Two-part epoxy paint
- Clear coating (optional)
- Flooring scraper
- Long-handled bristle brush
- Rented power scrubber
- Shop vacuum
- Respirator and rubber gloves
- Drill and stirring bit
- Paintbrush and paint roller
- Duct tape and painter's tape
- Plastic bag
- Paint stirrer
- Bucket

STEP-BY-STEP >>>

❶ **Before you buy the paint,** check to see if the concrete is too moist. Tape a plastic trash bag to the floor and wait 24 hours. Lift off the bag. If the area below is dry, apply the epoxy paint. If it's moist, wait. The moisture will not allow the paint to bond.

❷ **Use a flooring scraper** to remove hard gunk. If necessary, make concrete repairs as shown on pages 166-67. Remember that the paint will not smooth out any unevenness in the concrete surface.

❸ Pour a commercial degreasing solution over a 5x5-foot section. Equip a rented power scrubber with a brush attachment, and clean the section. Vacuum up the solution using a shop vacuum. Repeat until you've power-scrubbed the entire floor. Use a stiff bristle brush in corners where the power scrubber cannot reach.

❹ Pour a gallon of water into a plastic sprinkler can. Wearing a respirator, pour 2 cups of 32-percent muriatic acid (the most common type) into the water, to make a 1-to-8 etching solution. Mix with a paint stirrer, and pour over a 10x10-foot section. Scrub with a long-handled stiff bristle brush. Etch the entire floor this way. Rinse the floor three times to thoroughly flush out the residue, and allow the floor to dry overnight.

❺ Apply duct tape as needed to protect adjacent surfaces. Wearing a respirator and rubber gloves, pour the two parts of the epoxy paint into a bucket, and mix together using a drill and stirring bit. Follow the paint manufacturer's instructions; some recommend pouring the epoxy into a second bucket and mixing again.

❻ At the bottom of the garage door, apply duct tape to create a straight line. Brush a 4-inch-wide stripe against the tape, and also along the garage walls.

❼ Roll the paint in 4x4-foot areas. Apply first in a large "W" pattern, then roll straighter lines to fill in. Examine the surface closely, and work to remove any lines or globs made by the roller.

❽ Let the first coat dry according to the manufacturer's instructions. Before you apply the second coat, you may choose to add fine sand for a non-skid surface. Apply the second coat as you did the first. While it is still wet, you may choose to sprinkle the surface with color chips purchased with the paint. Allow to dry thoroughly, and perhaps add a clear top coat of a type recommended by the manufacturer.

CHAPTER 3

R eal estate pros often call the kitchen the most important room in the house. Whether you're fixing things up for your own satisfaction or with an eye toward resale, devote special attention to the room where you spend so much time and energy.

Kitchens are increasingly a gathering place as well as a workplace, so their surfaces should be able to stand up to close examination and hard use. Balancing those goals with budget considerations can be a challenge for anyone.

In this chapter, we'll look at low-cost opportunities to have a big impact on this vital room. In addition to the flooring options and painting techniques described earlier in this book, this chapter shows several ways to make a custom countertop and how to tile a backsplash.

Faucets and sinks can play a role far beyond their practical function. Replacements can be prominent style-setters for your new-look kitchen. Faucet sets today are usually packaged with hardware and tips for do-it-yourself installation. We'll talk you through the installation process, step by step.

Likewise, we'll show you how to install a new garbage disposer, hot-water dispenser, and water filter—appliances that may not be conspicuously visible but that will make your kitchen time more comfortable and enjoyable.

Saving on installation charges will make a modest budget go much further, and there's great satisfaction in knowing you did it yourself. Let's get started.

Updating Kitchens

Kitchen Faucet Replacement

You'll find many styles of kitchen faucets from which to choose. Some have separate sprayers, and single-control faucets have spouts that can be pulled out and used as sprayers.

If you're replacing your sink at the same time, you may have even more options. New sinks are typically predrilled for various faucet styles. If you'll be replacing a faucet on your current sink, go shopping armed with measurements and photos (above and below your faucet set) to ensure that your new faucet will fit and that you have appropriate hardware for your installation.

Manufacturers and retailers recognize the interests and needs of do-it-yourselfers. Plumbing connections are easier than in the past, and connection kits are available for most installations.

There are two possibilities for supply connections: Threaded inlets may be located directly below the hot and cold handles, or a pair of copper supply inlets may extend down from the center of the unit.

MATERIALS & TOOLS:

- Kitchen faucet
- Supply tubes (plastic or braided) long enough to reach the connections below
- Plumber's putty or caulk
- Basin wrench
- Slip-joint pliers
- Adjustable wrench
- Plastic putty knife
- Screwdriver
- Bucket and rags
- Paint thinner and cloth

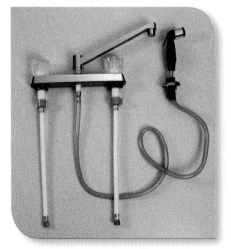

Two-Handle Faucet

Two-handle faucets have separate inlets below the handles and often have sprayers that attach at the center.

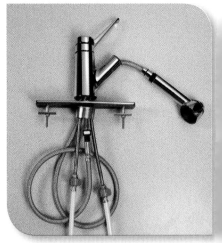

Single-Handle Faucet

Many newer single-control models have spouts that pull out to become sprayers. The inlets are copper tubes that extend down at the center.

STEP-BY-STEP >>>

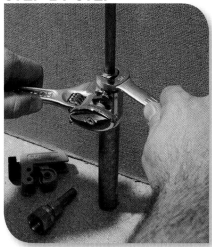

❶ From below, shut off the hot and cold stop valves leading to the faucet, and turn on the faucet to be sure the water is off. Use two wrenches or a pair of pliers and a wrench to loosen the nut holding the stop valves in place, and pull out the supply tube.

❷ Use a basin wrench to loosen and remove the nut or nuts that hold the faucet to the sink. To remove a two-handle faucet with separate inlets, as shown, loosen the large plastic nuts. If the faucet is a center-mount model, you may need to remove a center nut or two small nuts on either side. If there is a sprayer, disconnect it as well.

❸ From above, lift out the faucet. Scrape any old putty and collected grime using a plastic putty knife to avoid scratching the sink. Clean the sink with a cloth dampened with paint thinner. You may need to use a mineral cleaner as well.

Widespread Faucet

A "widespread" faucet does not have a flange that rests on the sink flange or countertop. Instead, the faucet and other components—perhaps one or two handles and a sprayer—emerge from separate holes in the countertop.

A widespread faucet does not have a baseplate, which creates a sleek modern look. The spout, handles, and sprayer all attach separately, giving them a distinctively different appearance.

TIP: SUPPLY TUBES AND MOUNTING METHODS

- You may be able to reuse the supply tubes from the old faucet, but measure to make sure they will reach to the stop valves. If you buy new supply tubes, check that they will fit the stop valves, which will be either ⅜ inch or ½ inch.

- Mounting methods vary from model to model. Read the manufacturer's instructions. Many one-handle faucets have a single mounting stud in the middle; slip a C-shaped clip onto the stud, then thread and tighten a nut to secure it.

- To install a two-handle faucet, connect the supply tubes, then press the faucet into place. Slip mounting nuts over the supply tubes and up to the faucet, and tighten with a basin wrench.

Kitchen Faucet Replacement

(Continued from previous page)

(Continued from previous page)

TIP: BASIN WRENCH

You won't use a basin wrench for anything else, but it is indispensable for removing and installing faucets. The wrench has a long handle and a swivel head that easily reaches a nut in a tight space. When you start turning, the jaws of the wrench clamp onto the nut. Flip the jaws over to change its function from tightening to loosening.

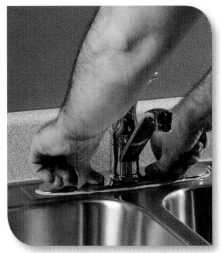

❹ Attach and tighten the supply tubes on the new faucet. Slip the faucet in place, and check that the tubes will reach the stop valves. Some faucets have a plastic flange that seals the plate to the sink. With other models, you must apply a bead of silicone caulk or a rope of plumber's putty to make the seal. Press the faucet firmly in place and check that it is centered and parallel with the edge of the sink.

❺ Have a helper hold the faucet in position while you crawl underneath to make the connections. On a two-handle faucet, screw a mounting nut onto each supply inlet and tighten with a basin wrench. If you have a one-handle faucet, follow the manufacturer's instructions for slipping on a washer, then threading and tightening one or more nuts. Have your helper check that the faucet is correctly aligned before you finish tightening.

TIP: FINAL TESTING PROCEDURE

With the stop valves still off, turn the faucet to the off position, and unscrew the aerator or spray head at the end of the spout. Then turn on the stop valves and turn on the hot and cold valves of the faucet. Run water for about a minute to remove debris in the lines. Turn off the faucet and reinstall the aerator or spray head. Turn the water back on and check for leaks below.

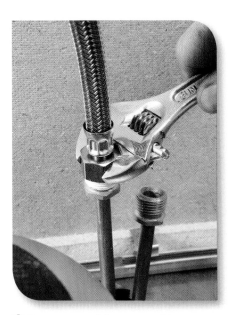

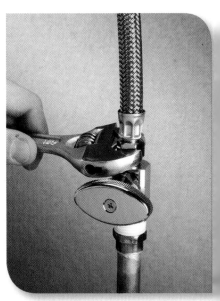

❻ On some models you need to connect the supply tubes after the mounting nut. First tighten by hand, then use a wrench. If you have copper inlets, use two wrenches—one to keep the copper inlet from twisting as you tighten the tube with the other wrench.

❼ Hand-tighten the supply tubes to the stop valves. Make sure Hot is on the left and Cold is on the right. Finish tightening using a wrench. Turn on the water and test for leaks; you may need to tighten some nuts more firmly.

STEP-BY-STEP >>> Installing a Sprayer

❶ **Clean the area around the sprayer** hole. Insert the sprayer's mounting flange into the hole. You may need to apply a rope of putty to the underside of the flange. Press down firmly to create a good seal.

❷ **From below, slip on the mounting flange's nut,** and tighten with a basin wrench. From above, clean away any squeezed-out putty. Thread the sprayer's hose down through the flange.

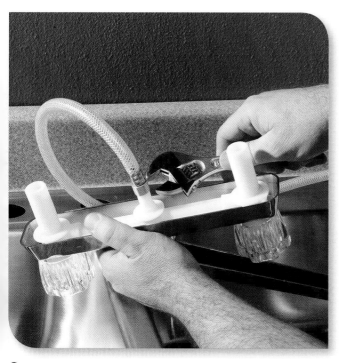

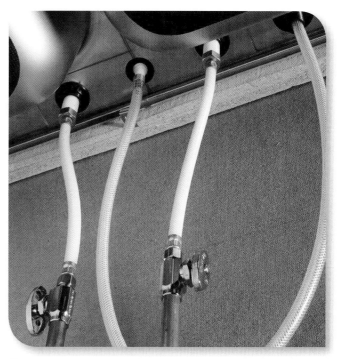

❸ **From below, thread the sprayer's hose** up through the center faucet hole. Screw it on the faucet's diverter and tighten with a wrench. In some cases, the faucet comes without the diverter installed; you have to install it before you connect the sprayer.

❹ **Seat the faucet and install it. From below, position the sprayer hose** so it will not get tangled when you pull the sprayer out. Connect and tighten the supply tubes to the shutoff valves. Turn on the water and inspect for leaks.

Painted Cabinets

Breathe new life into old cabinets with paint. The cost will be a tiny fraction of the price of new cabinets, and your kitchen will gain a unique, custom appearance.

First, decide if your cabinets are paintworthy: Do the drawers slide smoothly? Do the doors open and close easily? If not, perhaps call in a carpenter for repairs. If the stiles—the parts where the hinges attach and that drawers close against—are made of solid wood and are firmly attached, hinges and other hardware can be repaired.

Consider changing your hardware, too. New drawer pulls and door handles or knobs can refresh the overall look of a kitchen. Just be sure the new parts will fit into or cover the holes left when you remove the old ones.

MATERIALS & TOOLS:

- Primer and cabinet paint
- Drill and screwdriver
- Sanding block with 120-grit sandpaper
- Deglossing liquid
- Drop cloths and painter's tape
- Paintbrushes, rollers, and paint tray

STEP-BY-STEP >>>

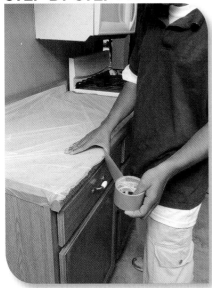

❶ Clean and rinse the cabinets thoroughly. Cover the nearby floor and countertops to protect them from spatters.

❷ Use a screwdriver to remove handles and knobs. You may choose to remove doors as well (see next page). Sand all the surfaces using a sanding block with 120-grit sandpaper, or brush with deglossing liquid. (Apply deglosser in small sections, so you can paint within an hour of deglossing.)

❸ Decide what you will paint. It's usually best to paint the back sides of doors, but painting interiors is optional. Apply painter's tape to hinges. Paint the backs of the doors with a brush, or brush-paint the perimeter and around the hinges and then go over the whole area with a roller.

❹ While the door backs are drying, brush-paint the exposed stiles and the front edges of shelving.

❺ Once the backs of doors are dry, partially close them and paint the door fronts. Then paint the stiles and rails of the frame. Pay attention to your brush strokes, which will be noticeable. Finish with long, straight strokes, and paint the longest pieces last.

❻ Tape the wall around the cabinets, and brush-paint the edges. Finish by painting with a roller, working to maintain a consistent surface texture with no noticeable lines.

Removing and Painting Doors

You may find it easiest to remove the doors first, especially if you will be replacing the hinges anyway. Use a drill with a screwdriver bit to remove the doors and hinges. Place the doors on short pieces of wood to raise them above a drop cloth for painting.

If a door has ornate moldings, use a flexible sponge sanding block to get into the crevices.

A narrow door with moldings cannot be successfully roller-painted. Work carefully with a good-quality brush. First fill all the edges, then go over the surface with long, light strokes to achieve a consistent finish.

Tile Countertops

Because tiles are available in so many colors, shapes, and styles, tiling a countertop allows you to create a very distinctive look. A tiled top does call for a bit more maintenance than a solid surface; mainly, you need to seal the grout every year or so—a process that takes less than a half hour. Still, tile is a durable surface that is easy to keep clean.

Be sure to use tiles made for countertops or floors; wall tiles are not strong enough and will crack. Exposed edges call for specialized tiles or edging treatments (see "Edging Options" at right).

Use latex- or polymer-reinforced grout. Also take care in choosing the plastic spacers that determine the width of the grout lines. Narrow spacers, perhaps $^3/_{16}$ inch, usually look best with 4- or 6-inch tiles; larger $^1/_4$-inch spacers are commonly used with 8- or 12-inch tiles.

If you plan to tile the backsplash, do it at the same time as the countertop. Here we show tiling a short backsplash. For a taller counter-to-wall-cabinet backsplash, see pages 82–83.

To start, disconnect the plumbing lines and remove the sink. Most laminate countertops are attached with screws driven up through the cabinet frame. Remove the screws and pull the top out.

MATERIALS & TOOLS:
- Tile ensemble: field tiles, trim tiles for edges and around a sink
- Grout and plastic spacers
- Sink with attaching hardware
- 3/4-inch plywood
- 1/2-inch cement backerboard
- Plastic sheeting, 4 mil or thicker
- Decking screws and backerboard screws
- Framing square and pencil
- Thinset mortar
- Power mortar
- Drill
- Snap tile cutter and rented wet saw to cut corners and curves
- Laminated grout float
- Sponge
- Staple gun
- Painter's tape
- Paper template for sink placement
- Jigsaw or circular saw
- Notched trowel
- Beater block and hammer
- Grout sealer

Edging Options

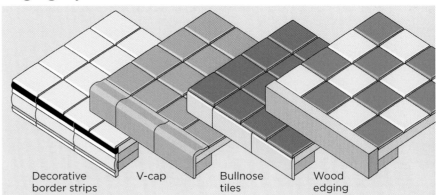

Decorative border strips | V-cap | Bullnose tiles | Wood edging

The edging is an integral part of the counter, so plan for it carefully. In most cases, the edging is installed first, then the field tiles. V cap is the most common choice because it provides a firm edging as well as a slight upturn at the corner, to keep water from spilling onto the floor. If you finish with bullnose pieces on the top, they should overhang the right distance so you can tuck edging tiles or border strips directly below. If you plan to install wood edging, run the field tiles just up to the edge, and provide ample backing so you can firmly attach the wood.

Subsurface

A tile top's subsurface should be very firm. Because a small amount of moisture can travel through grout lines, it must also be waterproofed. At right, a cutaway shows the usual configuration from bottom to top: Plywood; plastic sheeting; concrete backerboard; thinset mortar; and the tiles.

STEP-BY-STEP >>>

❶ Cut and install sheets of ¾-inch plywood for the bottom substrate layer. The plywood should overhang the cabinets by about 2 inches. Drive decking screws through the plywood and into the supporting cabinet frame every 4 inches or so.

❷ Cut sheets of 4 mil or thicker plastic, and staple securely to the plywood substrate.

❸ Cut backerboard (see pages 40–41) so solid pieces span the seams of the plywood. Drive 1¼-inch backerboard screws in a grid, with screws spaced no more than 6 inches apart. Drive 2-inch screws where they will attach to the cabinet's framing. Make sure all screw heads are sunk below the surface.

Layout Lines

Draw or snap layout lines for the trim tiles. A simple countertop needs just one line, for the front trim tiles. If there is a sink that is not self-rimming, you also need layout lines for the trim tiles around the sink. You'll position all your tiles in a dry run based on these lines. Layout lines and dry-run stages are covered in the step-by-step instructions on pages 78–79.

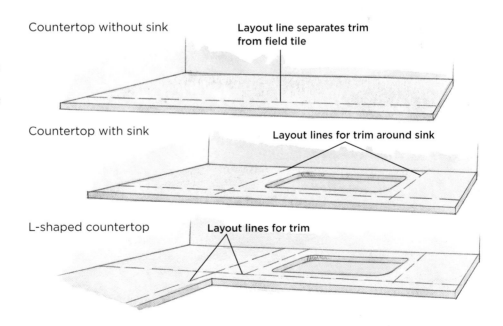

Countertop without sink

Layout line separates trim from field tile

Countertop with sink

Layout lines for trim around sink

L-shaped countertop

Layout lines for trim

Tile Countertops

(Continued from previous page)

❹ Draw guide lines for the trim tiles. If the counter is L-shaped, start in the corner. Be sure to take the width of the grout lines into account. Also keep in mind the thickness of any tiles installed on the edge (plus ¼ inch for the mortar that will attach them).

❺ Determine where the sink will fit; make sure it will not bump into any cabinet framing. Use a paper template provided by the manufacturer, or place the sink upside down on the backerboard and trace its outline; then draw the actual cutout line, about 1 inch inside the traced line.

❻ Drill holes at the corners of the sink cutout area. Cut with a jigsaw, or use a circular saw. Because a circular saw throws up a cloud of dust when cutting backerboard, have a helper hold a vacuum near the blade as shown. If you use a jigsaw, equip it with rough-cutting blades, and have extras on hand. If the sink will be flush-mounted or underhung, install it now. If it will be self-rimming, test to make sure it will fit, and plan to install it after tiling.

Sink Options

If you will be installing a sink, buy it beforehand and plan how you will install it before you set the tiles. A self-rimming sink is the easiest to install: Set field tiles around the opening, and add the sink after grouting.

A flush-mounted sink should have a rim that is thicker than the tiles. Install it before tiling, then run tiles up to its edge. These tiles will need to be cut precisely.

An underhung sink is the most difficult, but this style makes it easy to wipe crumbs and water into the sink. Install the sink, then add narrow bullnose tiles around the edge. Also install bullnose tiles around the opening.

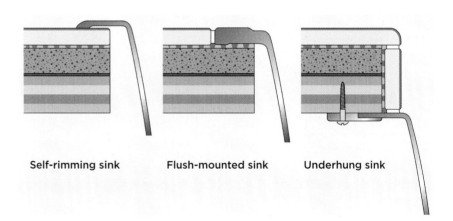

Self-rimming sink   Flush-mounted sink   Underhung sink

❼ Lay out the tiles in a dry run, using spacers for the grout lines. Check that all lines are straight. Once you do this, you may decide to adjust the layout in order to avoid ending up with narrow tiles at the front or the back. To be safe, do a dry run of the entire counter. As you work on the following steps, cutting and installing tiles, you may choose to remove only a portion of the dry-laid tiles, set them, and then move on to the next section.

❽ To mark a tile for cutting at the wall, place the tile to be cut directly on top of the next-to-last tile. Place another full tile on top, two grout lines away from the wall. Use the top tile to mark the cut line.

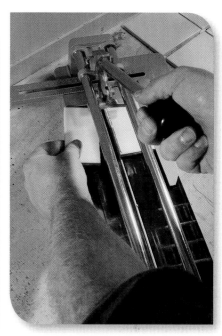

❾ Use a snap cutter for straight cuts. Because many tiles will be cut to the same size, use the cutter's guide to make multiple cuts.

Backsplash Options

If you will have only a short backsplash, it usually works best to use the same tiles as on the countertop, and to align the grout lines on both surfaces. Install a simple backsplash using bullnose tiles attached directly to the wall and resting on top of the counter's field tiles. For a more substantial look, attach a strip of backerboard or plywood to the wall, and make the backsplash with a field tile and a cap at the top. For a smooth transition that is easy to wipe clean, install cove tile against the wall and bullnose above it. Install the cove tiles before laying the counter's field tiles.

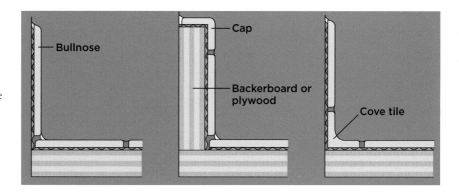

Tile Countertops

(Continued from previous page)

(Continued from previous page)

STEP-BY-STEP >>> Laying the Tile

❶ **Mix a batch** of latex- or polymer-reinforced thinset mortar according to the manufacturer's directions. Spread with the flat side of a notched trowel, then use the notched side to comb the surface of the mortar, slightly scraping the backerboard as you comb. Do not cover any layout lines.

❷ **Set the tiles along the layout lines,** slightly twisting and pressing each one. Use plastic spacers to maintain consistent grout lines. From time to time press a straightedge against a row of tiles to be sure the lines are straight.

❸ **Use a beater block**—a short 2x4 or 2x6 with carpet stapled to it—and a hammer to bed the tiles. Move the beater block over the surface and tap with the hammer as you go. Clean any squeezed-out mortar or mortar that comes near the tile surface.

❹ **When you come to edging** bullnose pieces or V-caps, back-butter them as needed so they rest in a good bed of mortar on the edge. You may need to tap with a beater block to achieve a straight edge, or remove a piece and add mortar as needed.

TIP: CUTTING EXPOSED CURVES

If you need to make a precise curve, buy a carbide hole saw made for cutting tile. It's basically a drill bit. Buy a bit that has the same radius as the curve you want to cut. Bore through the tile at the corner, then use a wet saw to cut between the curves.

Use a rented wet-cutting tile saw to make cutouts and curved cuts. Set the saw up so water sprays onto the blade at all times. Place the tile on the sliding table and slide it toward the blade to make the cut. To cut a curve, make a series of closely spaced cuts, then break the pieces out with tile nippers or your hand. Use the wet saw to scrape along the curve and smooth it out.

A thicker-looking backsplash is achieved by first applying a strip of backerboard or plywood to the wall, then setting radius bullnose pieces.

⑤ If backsplash tiles are the same size as countertop tiles, set them so the grout lines line up. These tiles do not get as much wear as the countertop tiles, so they can be set directly onto the wall. At an exposed corner you will need a corner cap, which has two bullnose edges.

⑥ Allow at least a day for the mortar to harden, then spread grout with a float held nearly flat to push grout into the joints. Next, tilt the float to scrape away the excess. Wipe several times with a damp sponge. Allow the grout to harden, then wipe with a clean, dry cloth to buff away any grout haze. Once the grout has cured, apply grout sealer.

Other Edgings

If you use bullnose countertop tiles instead of V cap, install the bullnose pieces so they overhang by the thickness of the edge pieces below, plus ¼ inch or so for the thickness of the mortar. Cut a number of edge pieces all to the same width, or use an edge strip, as shown. Back-butter the edge tile, and use masking tape to hold it in place until the mortar hardens.

To install wood edging, set the tiles to come within one grout line's thickness of the edge of the substrate. After the tiles are set, cut and attach the wood edging. Apply construction adhesive and drive trimhead screws into the plywood.

Tile Backsplash

The word "backsplash" can refer to a 3- to 5-inch-tall row of tiles or other material on the wall above a countertop; that type of backsplash is shown on page 79. Here we show a taller backsplash, one that usually runs from the counter up to the bottom of the wall cabinets.

Unlike counter tiles, backsplash tiles do not have to be particularly strong, so inexpensive wall tiles will do fine. If all the tiles in the top row will butt up against a wall cabinet, you need only field tiles. Where the top row will be exposed, buy bullnose tiles for a finished edge. You can attach them with thinset mortar or with tile mastic, which comes premixed. You may choose to continue up the wall using the same tiles as are on the counter, or you may choose backsplash tiles of contrasting color and style.

This is a quick and inexpensive way to dramatically spice up the look of a kitchen. With attractive tiles that coordinate with the counter, cabinets, and walls, this project can greatly improve the value of a kitchen.

MATERIALS & TOOLS:

- Tiles
- Plastic spacers
- Thinset mortar or wall tile mastic
- Snap cutter and tile nippers
- Wet saw, if needed
- Grout
- Tape measure
- Chalk line or pencil and straightedge
- Grout float
- Sponge
- Caulk
- Notched trowel

STEP-BY-STEP >>>

❶ Clean the wall and remove any electrical cover plates. If the tiles will continue the grout lines that are on the counter, set the bottom row of tiles in a dry run with plastic spacers. Mark the top edge and use a straightedge or a chalk line to make guide lines.

❷ Using a notched trowel, apply thinset mortar or tile mastic to the wall. Set the bottom row of tiles resting on plastic spacers. Where you meet an obstacle like an outlet or switch, use a wet saw or tile nippers to make cutouts.

❸ Allow the thinset or mastic a day to harden, then apply grout using a laminated grout float. Fill the joints, then squeegee away most of the waste. Use a damp sponge to gently clean the tiles and produce joints that are consistently just below the tile surface.

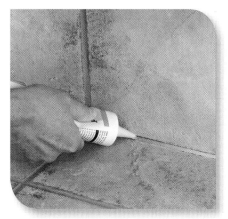

❹ Wipe the surface several times. Allow the grout to dry, then buff with a dry cloth. Fill the joint at the bottom with caulk that matches the grout color.

Glass Mosaic Tiles

Once expensive and unusual, glass tiles are now widely available and often inexpensively priced at home centers and tile stores. Some types have a muted pastel appearance, while others add splashes of vibrant color. Most often they come in mosaic sheets, which can be quickly installed and are easy to cut. The tiles shown below have a paper facing; other types have a mesh backing, which gets set into the mortar or mastic. Because the tiles are small, most cuts are made by removing whole tiles; where the tiles meet the underside of a cabinet, you can apply an extra-wide grout line and it will not be very visible. Use a utility knife to cut the paper facing or mesh backing. If you need to cut a tile, wear safety glasses and cut with a tile nipper.

Glass is somewhat translucent, so use a white thinset mortar or tile mastic, or a product recommended by your tile dealer. Consult the tile's information sheet and check with your tile dealer to choose either a sanded or a non-sanded grout; sanded grout can scratch some glass tiles. Use a notched trowel of the size recommended for your tile.

❶ Check the counter for level, and mark a level or parallel line one sheet's height above the counter. If the tiles are larger than 3 inches, use painter's tape to set the sheets in a dry run and plan the layout so there will not be a column of narrow slivers at either end.

❷ Use a notched trowel to apply thinset or mastic to the wall, and press the sheets into the tiles. Apply duct tape or painter's tape to hold the pieces in place. Allow for a joint's thickness between adjacent sheets.

❸ Peel back the facing if there is any, and wipe away any residue. Apply grout using a laminated grout float. Scrape away the excess, then very gently wipe with a damp sponge, cleaning the sponge often. Work to maintain joints of consistent depth. Wipe several times. Allow to dry, then buff with a dry cloth.

Kitchen Sinks

This project can be challenging, so study your sink's plumbing before you start. If you run into an unusual plumbing situation, you may choose to hire a professional plumber for the installation. But if the basic under-sink plumbing—the drain pipe and the stop valves for the supply lines—is in place, installing a sink is a fairly straightforward do-it-yourself project. If you are replacing a sink that was working well, leave as many plumbing parts as possible on it and use it as a guide for installing the new plumbing. The illustrations here show the most common drain arrangements.

If you are also installing a new countertop, see pages 78 and 112 for information on cutting holes for sinks.

A self-rimming sink, shown in the steps on the following pages, is the simplest installation. But an under-mounted sink is an appealing option because it makes it easier to clean the counter (see page 98).

MATERIALS & TOOLS:

- Kitchen sink to fit in the counter's hole
- Faucet
- Garbage disposer with appliance extension cord
- Trap assembly made of 1½-inch parts
- Supply tubes
- Flexible line and air gap for dishwasher
- Sawhorses
- Plumber's putty
- Drop cloth
- Drill
- Screwdriver
- Groove-joint pliers
- Adjustable wrench
- Strainer wrench or spud wrench
- Hacksaw
- Cable clamp and hose clamps
- Mounting clips
- Caulk

Sink Assembly

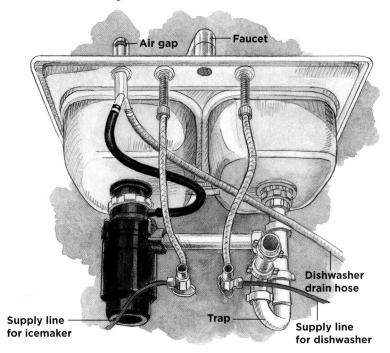

Air gap · Faucet · Supply line for icemaker · Trap · Dishwasher drain hose · Supply line for dishwasher

Alternate Trap Configurations

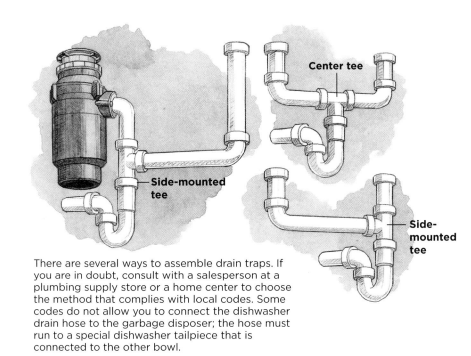

Center tee · Side-mounted tee · Side-mounted tee

There are several ways to assemble drain traps. If you are in doubt, consult with a salesperson at a plumbing supply store or a home center to choose the method that complies with local codes. Some codes do not allow you to connect the dishwasher drain hose to the garbage disposer; the hose must run to a special dishwasher tailpiece that is connected to the other bowl.

Kitchen Sink Strainers

A basket strainer attaches to a sink's drain hole with a locknut below. A fiber washer and a rubber washer ensure a tight but flexible attachment. A tailpiece with a plastic washer attaches to the underside of the strainer.

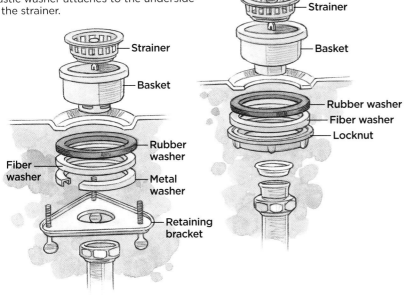

- Strainer
- Basket
- Rubber washer
- Fiber washer
- Metal washer
- Retaining bracket

- Strainer
- Basket
- Rubber washer
- Fiber washer
- Locknut

STEP-BY-STEP >>> Basket Strainer Installation

❶ **Place the sink on a pair of sawhorses** so you can work above and under the sink. To install a basket strainer, make a rope of plumber's putty and press it onto the strainer's flange. Press the strainer into the hole.

❷ **From below, slip on the rubber washer,** then the fiber washer, and tighten the locknut. Use pliers and a screwdriver, as shown, to hold the strainer in place while you or a helper uses a strainer wrench or spud wrench to tighten the locknut from below.

3

TIP: CHOOSING A SINK

When it comes to sinks, you generally get what you pay for.

- An inexpensive stainless-steel sink scratches more easily, is difficult to keep clean, is noisy when water runs onto it, and flexes when you push on it. A higher-quality model uses stronger steel (16 or 18 gauge) and has a sleek, burnished finish. Make sure the underside is coated with sound-deadening insulation.

- An enameled cast-iron sink will last longer than an enameled steel sink and has a more solid feel. A cast-iron sink is more durable than a steel sink and has sound-deadening properties.

- Acrylic sinks look like cast-iron, but they are not as durable and are prone to scratching.

- Cast-iron and acrylic sinks keep water warm longer than stainless-steel or enameled steel sinks.

TIP: ASSEMBLING A TRAP

Plastic traps are now more popular than chrome-plated steel in places where they will not be visible. Plastic lasts forever and is easier to cut and assemble. You will need a slip washer and a nut for each joint. Where a tailpiece attaches to a strainer, you will need a special plastic washer. To cut plastic pipe, use a fine-toothed saw.

Kitchen Sinks

(Continued from previous page)

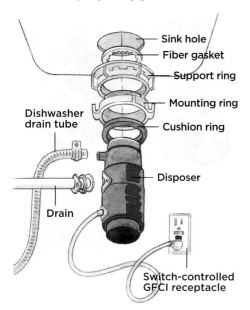

- Sink hole
- Fiber gasket
- Support ring
- Mounting ring
- Cushion ring
- Dishwasher drain tube
- Disposer
- Drain
- Switch-controlled GFCI receptacle

A garbage disposer plugs into a switch-controlled outlet. Once the flange and support ring are installed, the disposer is twisted into position.

STEP-BY-STEP >>> Installing a Garbage Disposer

❶ **Turn the sink upside down** if you are installing a garbage disposer on a new sink. Push the flange up through the hole. Slip on the gasket and screw on the mounting ring (see the illustration at left). Use a strainer wrench or spud wrench to tighten the ring.

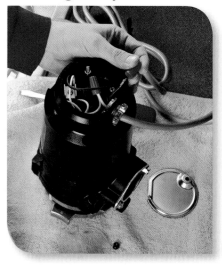

❷ **Following the manufacturer's instructions,** remove the disposer's electrical cover plate. Install a cable clamp, run an appliance extension cord through it, and strip the wire ends to make the electrical connections. Secure the connections with wire nuts. Replace the cover plate.

❸ **Slide the mounting ring over the flange.** Install the cushion mount, making sure the groove on the inside fits over the lip of the sink flange. Position the disposer over the flange, push down, and twist until the disposer is anchored.

❹ **Assemble the trap** (see the illustrations on page 84). For an installation like this one, slip the tailpiece's plastic washer into the basket strainer and tighten a nut to attach the tailpiece to the strainer. Add the T fitting and the arm that attaches to the disposer. Then install the trap. Be sure to use washers at each joint. The arm coming from the trap leads to the drain pipe in the wall; you may need to cut the arm to fit or add an extension.

❺ **If you need to install a dishwasher drain,** it is a good idea to add an air gap fitting, as shown. Attach the air gap to a hole in the sink using a mounting nut. Use hose clamps to attach the hose that runs from the air gap to the disposer's tailpiece (see the illustration on page 108). You will attach the hose from the dishwasher later, when you install the sink.

6 Install the faucet while the sink is inverted. Follow the faucet-installation instructions shown on pages 70–73.

7 Screw flexible supply tubes onto the faucet inlets. Make sure they are long enough to reach the stop valves, and that they are the same size as the stop valves (either ⅜ inch or ½ inch). If the faucet has flexible copper inlets, use two wrenches or pliers to avoid twisting and kinking the inlets.

8 Lower the sink into the hole and go below to check that the tubes and trap parts will fit; you may need to make some adjustments. Remove the sink. For a steel sink, place a rope of putty under the sink's flange or along the perimeter of the counter hole. Lower the sink onto the putty.

9 A cast-iron sink is heavy enough to stay in place with just some added caulk. For other sinks, slide mounting clips onto the sink's channels, slide them over, turn them so they grab the underside of the countertop, and tighten the screws. There should be a clip every 8 inches or so.

10 Hook up the supply tubes to the stop valves and tighten with pliers. Run the trap's arm into the trap adapter in the wall and tighten the connection. Tighten all the trap connections.

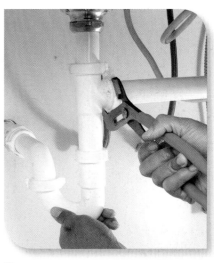

11 Some plastic traps can be tightened by hand, but then give an extra quarter-turn with a pair of groove-joint pliers. Open the stop valves and test the faucet. Stop up both bowls and fill about three-fourths full of water, then unstop the bowls and check for leaks. Tighten joints as needed.

Hot-Water Dispenser

A hot-water dispenser instantly provides water that is near the boiling point. You can use it to brew tea, melt chocolate, make gravy, cook thin asparagus—and on and on. Many newer models, like the ones shown here, have sleek styles that elegantly complement almost any kitchen faucet.

In addition to supplying very hot water, some dispensers allow you to mix in cold water, so you can instantly have water that is just the right temperature for washing your hands or scrubbing pots.

Installation is not difficult, as long as you have the following:

- An available hole in your sink or in the counter, for mounting the faucet.
- An electrical plug under the sink that is not controlled by a switch—it must be always "hot." If you don't have one, have an electrician install one for you. (In some cases there will be a two-plug receptacle under the sink that has one plug controlled by a switch for the garbage disposer and one plug that is always hot.)
- A nearby cold-water supply pipe that you can tap into.

A hot-water dispenser isn't a necessity in any kitchen, but once you have one you'll wonder how you got along without it. And as the photos show, a well-chosen dispenser can enhance the look of a sink.

MATERIALS & TOOLS:

- Hot-water dispenser
- Saddle tee valve (or T fitting and stop valve, if you are good at plumbing)
- Drill
- Adjustable wrench
- Groove-joint pliers
- Basin wrench

STEP-BY-STEP >>>

❶ **Using a saddle tee valve,** follow the manufacturer's instructions to clamp the valve onto a cold-water pipe near where you will mount the dispenser. There will be a rubber washer to seal the point where the valve enters the pipe. Tighten the clamps. You will later turn the valve's handle clockwise to puncture the pipe.

❷ **Thread the spout's copper water lines** down through a knockout hole. Have a helper hold the spout from above while you crawl underneath. Slip on a washer and mounting nut and tighten. If hand-tightening does not make it firm enough, use a basin wrench to tighten further.

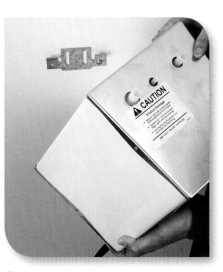

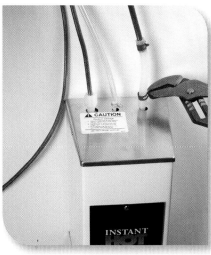

❸ Choose a location on the wall or a cabinet where the dispenser's water lines will easily reach. Screw on the mounting bracket, and slip the tank onto the bracket.

❹ Follow the manufacturer's instructions for connecting the lines. When working with copper, bend gently to avoid kinking the line. On this model, copper lines connect using a plastic nut and a ferrule. Plastic tubes are secured with squeeze clamps.

TIP: STYLES TO CHOOSE

Manufacturers now make hot-water dispensers to harmonize with most faucets and to suit any décor, so this feature can be attractive as well as convenient.

Other Valves

Though a screw-in saddle valve almost always works just fine, many plumbers prefer to install a saddle valve that requires first drilling a hole. For an even more secure connection, install a T fitting in the cold water line and add a new stop valve. Beware: Both of these methods require that you shut off the water to the pipe and test to make sure the water is off. If you are not experienced in this kind of plumbing work, call in a professional plumber.

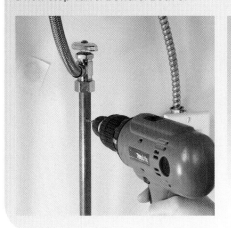

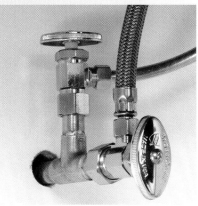

A hot-water dispenser's spout mounts through a hole in the sink or in the counter. The tank mounts onto a wall bracket and is plugged into an always-hot outlet. In this model, right, a copper tube runs from a saddle tee or other valve in the cold-water line and to the spout, and two other copper lines run to the tank. A plastic vent tube also connects to the tank.

Overview of Hot Water Dispenser Installation

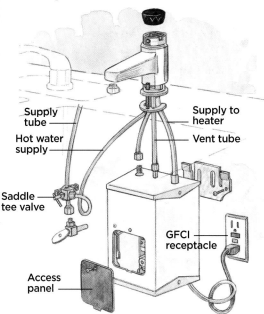

Supply tube
Supply to heater
Hot water supply
Vent tube
Saddle tee valve
GFCI receptacle
Access panel

Although it is a utilitarian and often small space, a bathroom presents a real opportunity for dramatic change on a budget. People love bathrooms that are cheery, bright, and uncluttered. So this chapter shows you how to install bathroom elements that positively gleam: wall tiles around the tub; new handles, spouts, and shower heads; a medicine cabinet; and towel racks, shelves, and grab bars. We'll also show more ambitious installations: a toilet and two kinds of sink. Combined with what the book already has shown about painting and flooring, you'll be equipped to change just about every square inch of a bathroom.

Because a bathroom is a small but important space, it often pays in the long run to spend more for high-quality fixtures and materials. Change the faucets and fixtures on the sink, tub, and shower to stylish models in popular finishes like satin or brushed nickel. Then upgrade your cabinet hardware, lighting fixtures, and mirror to complete the fresh look.

As any growing family or working couple will tell you, a second sink in a bathroom adds immeasurable value. If there's room for two sinks within 30 inches of each other, the two can share drainage and supply lines, which decreases costs.

And if you want just one new detail that you'll appreciate daily, a new showerhead can dramatically improve your morning routine. Consider installing a pan-style model that simulates a refreshing rain shower. You and your bath will both feel fresher.

Brightening Bathrooms

Tile Tub Surround

A round a tub with a showerhead, tile is commonly installed to a height of about 5 feet above the tub, which usually means about a half foot above the shower head. At the sides, extend the tile at least one vertical row of tiles past the tub wherever possible. Wherever the edges of the tiles will be exposed, install bullnose cap tiles, which have one curved finished edge. At an exposed corner (there are usually two in a tub surround), install corner tiles, also called down angles.

Tub tiles are sometimes installed onto water-resistant drywall, also called greenboard or blueboard, but cement backerboard is a much better option. Greenboard will rot if it gets wet, but cement backerboard will not. Organic mastic is easy to use because it's premixed, but thinset mortar is stronger and more moisture resistant. It may take a bit of practice to mix at the right consistency—as wet as possible, but dry enough to hold the troweled comb shapes.

Tiling a tub surround can really enhance the perception and value of a bathroom. Simple designs, often with a band or two of different-colored tiles, are the most popular. It is important that the tiles be installed to form a smooth surface, with no protruding corners, and that all the corners meet neatly.

MATERIALS & TOOLS:

- Roofing felt and roofing cement
- Stapler and staples
- Cement backerboard, mesh tape, and backerboard screws
- Silicone caulk
- Field tiles
- Bullnose and corner tiles
- Soap dish or other accessory
- Painter's tape
- Level and straight board for batten
- Mastic or thinset mortar
- Notched trowel
- Grout and grout float
- Grout saw
- Hammer and cold chisel
- Shims
- Drop cloth or heavy paper
- Snap cutter and nippers
- Rented wet saw, if needed
- Rod cutter
- Sponge

STEP-BY-STEP >>> Prepping the Walls

❶ **If there is existing tile,** use a grout saw to remove most of the grout, then chip out the tiles using a hammer and cold chiseon. Spread out a drop cloth to protect the tub from debris, and wear eye protection and gloves because sharp shards will fly around. If the underlayment is solid and smooth, you can reuse it; otherwise, remove and replace it with cement backerboard.

❷ **Remove any hardware** that may get in the way. You don't have to remove the showerhead's arm, but pry away the escutcheon. Remove the tub spout, as well as faucet handles and escutcheons.

Plan the layout so you do not end up with a narrow vertical row of tiles at either corner. On the sides you may need to extend the tiles more than a tile's width past the tub. On the back wall, plan to cut tiles on either side that are the same size, and that are more than half wide. To be certain of your layout, set a row of tiles on the tub, including spacers if you will be using them.

❸ **Many installers skip this step,** but it ensures against water damage to your framing. Spread roofing cement on the upper flange of the tub. Staple roofing felt to the studs, taking care not to rip the paper as you work. Overlap upper and lower pieces by at least 6 inches.

❹ **Cut backerboard as shown** on page 41. Place ¼-inch spacers on top of the tub, and set the backerboard on them. Drive backerboard screws to fasten to the studs. Reinforce the corners with fiberglass mesh tape. Skim-coat over the tape with thinset mortar, let dry, and sand smooth.

❺ **Remove the spacers** and fill the gap with silicone caulk. Caulk is flexible so that the tub can move when it fills and empties without damaging the tiles.

❻ **If the tub is perfectly level on all three sides,** tack a straight board, called a batten, a full tile's width plus ⅛ inch above the tub. If it is not perfectly level (which is usually the case), tack it level, three-fourths of a tile's width above the tub. Cover the tub with a drop cloth or heavy paper to protect it from dropped tiles and debris.

❼ **Make a dry run with tiles and spacers,** and locate a point near the middle where there will be a vertical grout line. Draw a level line at that point. Do this on all three walls.

Tile Tub Surround

(Continued from previous page)

STEP-BY-STEP >>> Setting the Tile

❶ **Mix a small batch of thinset mortar** so it is just barely dry enough to hold its shape. Using a notched trowel, first spread the mortar with the flat side, pressing as you go. Then comb with the notched side, holding the trowel at a consistent angle.

❷ **Set field tiles on the back wall first,** starting with the tiles that rest atop the batten. Every once in a while pull a tile back to make sure it is fully embedded in the mortar. If the mortar is starting to harden, scrape it off the wall and mix a new batch. When you install tiles on the side walls, start with the bullnose tiles at the front edge and move toward the corner, so all cut tiles are at the corners.

❸ **Once the mortar has hardened** enough to hold the tiles in place, remove the supporting batten. Cut and install tiles for the bottom row. Also install cut tiles at the corners and around fixtures. Use a snap cutter to make all straight cuts, and nippers, a rod cutter, or a wet saw to make notches and curved cuts (see page 80).

❹ **Leave spaces for any soap dishes** or other accessories. Cut a tile or two to fit around it. Spread mortar on the wall and back-butter the accessory. Hold it with tape until the mortar dries, then caulk the joint.

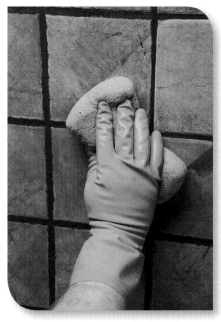

TIP: TILES AT THE TUB CORNERS

At each corner of the tub you will need to cut a tile at a curve that matches the tub. First cut a cardboard template, and use it to mark the tile (which may be a field tile or may be a bullnose tile). Cut slowly and carefully with a rod saw. It may take several attempts to get this just right.

⑤ **Allow the mortar to cure** at least overnight—longer if the air is humid. Clean away any mortar that is less than ¼ inch from the surface of the tiles. Mix latex-reinforced grout, unsanded for joints ⅛ inch or less and sanded for larger joints. Apply with a grout float. First hold the float nearly flat and force it into the joints, moving the float in at least two directions at all points. Then tilt the float up and squeeze away most of the excess grout. Hold the float at an angle to the joints so you don't dig in.

⑥ **Dampen a sponge and clean the surface** at least twice, continually rinsing the sponge in clean water. Smooth the joints as you work. If a gap appears, fill it with mortar and wipe again. Allow to dry, and wipe away the haze with a clean, dry rag.

Bullnose and Trim

Use bullnose or "cap" tile everywhere there is an exposed edge. At a corner, use a corner cap, also called a down angle, which has two finished edges. As you install the top row, wipe away excess thinset from the wall as you go. A band of "rope" trim, as shown, neatly frames the top of an installation.

Tub and Shower Fixtures

New chrome—or nickel or other finish—can put a gleam in your bathroom's eye. Because so many options are available, you may choose to update the look, go for a retro style, or just change one or two elements to achieve a more unified look.

Showerheads and tub faucets are fairly universal; you can install any brand just about anywhere, though you may need some adapting hardware. Handles and escutcheons are more manufacturer-specific; go to the store armed with the name of the manufacturer, or bring along a handle you want to replace in order to get one that will fit.

If you like the style of your existing shower fixtures except for the dingy factor, try cleaning them with a metal cleaner. If they still look bad, you'll make your bathroom more appealing if you replace them.

MATERIALS & TOOLS:

- Showerhead
- Shower arm
- Tub spout with adapters
- Handles to match
- Teflon tape
- Screwdriver
- Adjustable wrench
- Groove-joint pliers
- Pipe wrench

TIP: LOTS TO CHOOSE FROM

At a home center or hardware store you can find a good selection of spouts, handles, and showerheads.

Showerhead

If the showerhead is attached by a hex nut, use a wrench rather than pliers to remove and install. If the nut is round, use groove-joint pliers, and protect the metal against scratches with a covering of cloth or tape.

A shower arm is inexpensive, so replace yours if it looks dingy or if its finish does not match the new showerhead. Use a pipe wrench or groove-joint pliers, and protect the new arm with a cloth or tape.

STEP-BY-STEP >>>

❶ **Before twisting on a new showerhead** or a new shower arm, wrap two or three windings of Teflon tape clockwise around the threads.

❷ **Start twisting on the showerhead** with your fingers. It should turn two or more times with little resistance; if not, you may have cross-threaded, so back up and try again. Tighten with a wrench or cloth-protected pliers.

Tub Spout

Many spouts simply twist off but beware: If yours is attached to unthreaded copper pipe, there is a little setscrew on the bottom of the spout holding it in place. Scrunch yourself underneath to get a look, or use a mirror. You may need a hex (Allen) wrench to loosen the setscrew. Choose a new spout with the same kind of diverter, if any, as the old one.

This "universal" spout comes with adapters so it can fit onto any kind of pipe. Instructions show how to attach to short or long threaded pipes, or to unthreaded copper pipe.

❶ **Use a pipe wrench** or groove-joint pliers to remove the old spout. Measure the pipe that comes out from the wall and use the adapter that fits the situation.

❷ **Wrap the threaded end of the pipe** with two or three clockwise windings of Teflon tape. Twist the spout first by hand. If it doesn't turn a couple of times easily, back up and try again, to avoid cross-threading.

❸ **Protect the spout from scratches** by wrapping it with a cloth. Tighten it with a pipe wrench or large groove-joint pliers. Ideally the spout should tighten firmly just when it reaches the wall. If not, try using a different adapter or removing the spout and adding more windings of Teflon tape.

Handles

❶ **If you have a one-handle control,** pry out the plastic cap and unscrew the mounting screw. Pull the handle off.

❷ **The escutcheon usually mounts** with two screws. If you install a new escutcheon, be sure the foam or rubber gasket attaches firmly against the tiles all around to keep water out.

Bathroom Faucets

Most bathroom faucets fit into sinks with three holes spaced 4 inches apart (from the center of the left hole to the center of the right hole). In addition to installing the faucet, you will need to attach the pop-up stopper assembly. Many bathroom faucets now come with new drain bodies (see page 100).

Removal and replacement are pretty straightforward, but you may find yourself working in a cramped space, especially if the sink sits on a vanity. If you have a pedestal sink that is well attached to a wall bracket (see pages 108–109), you may be able to slide the pedestal out to gain more working space. Clear the area and place thick towels on the floor for comfort; either position your tools within easy reach or have a helper on hand to give you tools as you need them.

Choose a faucet style that harmonizes with the bathroom's towel bars, shower hardware, and other features.

MATERIALS & TOOLS:
- Bathroom faucet, perhaps with new drain body
- Plumber's putty and pipe-thread tape
- Trap gaskets or a new trap
- Screwdriver
- Adjustable wrench
- Groove-joint pliers
- Putty knife
- Basin wrench
- Bucket

TIP: SHUT OFF THE WATER!

Before you start, be sure the water has been shut off (you want a new faucet, not a fountain). Usually you will find two stop valves, also called fixture shutoff valves, under the sink. One is for hot and the other for cold water. Turn the valves clockwise and tighten them shut. Open the faucet to make sure the water is completely shut off. If there are no valves, or if they do not shut off the water, don't proceed; call in a professional plumber.

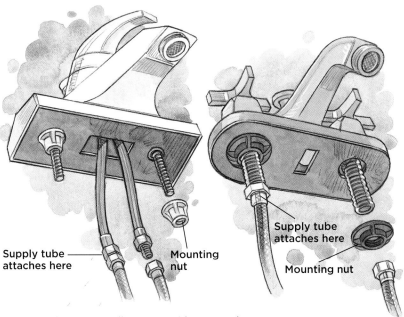

Supply tube attaches here

Mounting nut

Supply tube attaches here

Mounting nut

Bathroom faucets usually mount with nuts at the two outside holes. On a single-handle model (above, left) copper supply tubes run through the center hole and mounting nuts are on each side. A two-handle faucet (above, right) has mounting nuts below the handles.

STEP-BY-STEP >>>

1 Place a bucket under the trap—the chrome or plastic pipes that are shaped like a sideways "P." Using groove-joint pliers, loosen the nut on each side of the curved trap piece. Slide the nuts out of the way and pull the curved piece out. (Don't be surprised if you find hair and other gunk that needs to be cleaned out.)

2 Shut off the hot and cold stop valves, and open the faucet to be sure the water is shut off. Use a basin wrench to disconnect the supply tubes just below the faucet, or disconnect them at the stop valves. Remove the mounting nuts. Loosen the setscrew that holds the clevis strap to the pivot rod (see the illustration below, pinch the clip, and slide the clevis strap off.

3 Pull the old faucet out and clean the top of the sink. On a single-handled faucet you can connect the supply tubes to the faucet at this point. Slip on the rubber gasket, if one is supplied; if not, apply a rope of putty, as shown. Lower the faucet and press it into place.

4 Have a helper hold the faucet while you tighten the mounting nuts from below. You may need to use a basin wrench to firmly tighten the nuts. Also attach and tighten the supply tubes.

A pop-up drain assembly has several working parts. A pivot rod inserts into the tailpiece, where a plastic ball enables it to move while a gasket and nut seal out water. The rod connects to a clevis strap, which attaches to a lift rod, so you can raise and lower the stopper from above.

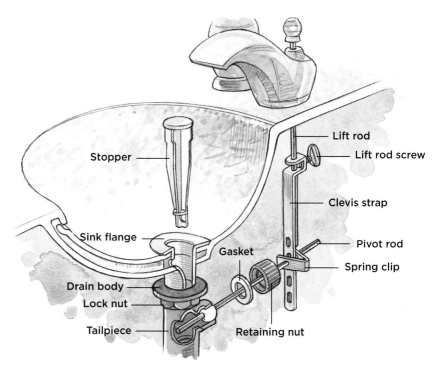

Bathroom Faucets

(Continued from previous page)

⑤ You can use the existing drain body (whose flange appears at the sink hole), or you may choose to install a new drain body (see below). With the stopper closed, slide the clevis strap onto the lift rod, using the metal clip to hold it in place. Test to see that you can effectively raise and lower the stopper from above; if not, insert the pivot rod into a different hole in the clevis strap, or slide the strap up or down. Tighten the setscrew that holds the clevis strap onto the lift rod.

⑥ If the old trap parts look worn, take them to your retailer and buy replacement parts to match. You may need to cut the arm piece (which comes after the curved piece and typically travels into the wall) with a hacksaw. Reassemble the trap: Slip on nuts, then rubber or plastic gaskets, taking care to keep them straight. Slide the curved piece onto the two other pieces, slide the gaskets down to seat them, and screw on the nuts. Tighten with groove-joint pliers. Turn the water back on and test for leaks.

TIP: TRAP TIPS

- Even if your metal trap parts are in good shape and you will reuse them, it is a good idea to replace the rubber or plastic gaskets, which wear out easily. Take the old gaskets to a plumbing supply source and buy exact replacements.

- If you don't mind the look, a plastic (PVC) trap is easier to install, cheaper, and actually lasts longer. Consult with your plumbing dealer; you may be able to replace some or all of the old metal parts with plastic.

- Test for leaks carefully: Close the stopper and open the faucet to fill the bowl at least halfway. Then open the stopper and watch underneath for leaks. In most cases, tightening nuts will stop leaks. If not, you may need to reassemble the parts.

Replacing a Drain Body

① Loosen the slip nut to disconnect the drain body from the trap. Remove the locknut under the sink, and slide out the old drain body. Clean the area around the hole. Place a rope of putty onto the new drain flange, and press the flange into the hole.

② While holding the flange tight from above (you may need a helper), work from below to slip the washer and rubber gasket, then thread the locknut and tighten with groove-joint pliers. Keep the drain body's hole facing to the rear.

③ Apply pipe-thread tape to the threaded end of the tailpiece, and screw it onto the drain body. Attach the pop-up assembly and the trap.

Hand Showers

A hand shower adds convenience and luxury—and can give a bathroom a bit of high-tech or old-fashioned pizzazz, depending on the style you choose. The showerhead will spend most of its life resting in a bracket and behaving like a regular showerhead, but its mobility makes it great for washing young children and even the family dog.

Replacing a Plain Showerhead

If you already have a showerhead, buy a unit with a diverter that attaches to the shower arm. Use slip-joint pliers to remove the existing showerhead (see page 96). You may choose to replace the shower arm as well. Clean the threads, and screw the unit's bracket onto the shower arm by hand. There is no need to use Teflon tape. Screw the hose onto the showerhead and onto the bracket in the same way. Turn on the water to test. If there is a leak, use pliers to give the fitting an extra half-turn.

Installing a Hand Shower without a Prior Showerhead

If you have a tub without a shower, installing a hand shower is the easiest way to add one. Or install it low on the wall to use it as a hand shower only. Buy a unit that includes a replacement spout, a showerhead with a hose, and a bracket for attaching the head.

Remove the existing spout (see pages 96–97) and install the new one. Screw the hose's fitting onto the underside of the spout. With most units there is no need for Teflon tape. You may need to use pliers, but avoid overtightening.

Some showerhead brackets have self-sticking backs. Go ahead and mount one this way, but you may find that it comes off and you need to attach it with screws. Clean the wall thoroughly. Hold the hanger in place and mark for the screw holes. Use a hammer and a nail to lightly nick the tile so the drill bit does not wander. Equip a drill with a masonry bit of the recommended size, and drill through the tile. Push plastic anchors into the holes. Attach the bracket with screws driven into the anchors.

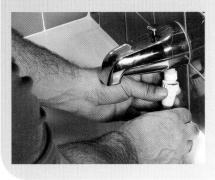

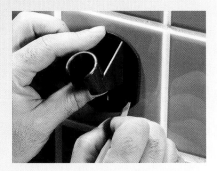

Towel Racks and Grab Bars

Small upgrades can be inexpensive, beneficial, and satisfying. Take these simple examples: a new towel rack and a grab bar. Regardless of what style you select, most basic bathroom shelves and towel racks install similarly, either with visible screws driven into the wall or with a hidden screwed-on bracket. Read the manufacturer's instructions for the details.

Though these installations are often advertised as easy, some items can be a bit tricky. The important things, of course, are keeping racks and shelves perfectly level and mounting them securely. The best attachment is a long screw driven directly into a wall stud. Second best is a toggle bolt, described in the tip box below. For one end of the lightweight towel rack project, we used a simple wall anchor.

MATERIALS & TOOLS:
- Towel rack, shelf, or grab bar
- Toggle bolts
- Long screws to reach studs (if not supplied by the manufacturer)
- Stud finder
- Drill and bits, including masonry bit
- Screwdriver and jeweler's screwdriver
- Masking tape
- Hammer
- Level and tape measure
- Plastic or metal wall anchors
- Silicone caulk

TIP: TOGGLE BOLTS

Toggle bolts are stronger than plastic anchors, though not as strong as screws driven into studs. To install one, drill a hole the recommended size. Slip the bolt through the fixture's or bracket's hole, and start to screw on the toggle's nuts, which have spring-loaded wings. Fold the wings down and slip the bolts through the holes until the wings snap open inside the wall. When you tighten the nuts, the wings grab the back side of the wall, for a firm connection.

STEP-BY-STEP >>> Towel Rack

❶ Tape the rack's pieces together so they stay in alignment as you work. Hold the rack in place and mark the centers of the escutcheons. Also check for level.

❷ Hold each mounting bracket in place and mark for two screw holes. Keep the bracket plumb (straight up and down) as you mark.

❸ If you were able to locate the bracket over a stud, fasten by driving screws, at least 1¼ inches long, into the studs. If not, drill a hole the size recommended by the anchor manufacturer.

❹ Tap a plastic or metal wall anchor into each hole. The anchor should fit snugly.

TIP: ATTACH TO STUDS

For the strongest attachment, drive screws into wall studs. To find the studs, use an electronic stud finder, which senses the presence of wood behind drywall. If you will attach to a tiled wall, look for a stud above the tiles and use a level to locate the spot directly below on the tiles. If you can't find studs, use hollow wall anchors (see step 2 below) or toggle bolts.

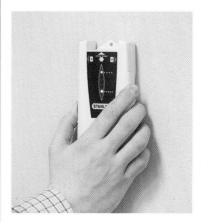

⑤ Drive screws into the anchors to attach the brackets. Most require only a simple screwdriver; some commercial models may include screws that require an allen wrench.

⑥ Place the towel rack's escutcheons over the brackets. If they don't push flush to the wall, you may need to loosen the setscrews at the bottom. Hold the rack firmly against the wall as you tighten the setscrew. The rack may include a hex wrench that fits the setscrew, or (as here) you may need to use a little jeweler's screwdriver.

STEP-BY-STEP >>> Grab Bar

① Use a stud finder to locate studs. Hold the bar in position and mark for holes; aim to have at least two of the screws driven into a stud. When drilling through ceramic tile, use a masonry bit and cover the area with masking tape to prevent cracking. Drill a 1/8-inch pilot hole first, then the larger hole for the screw or an anchor.

② Where you cannot reach a stud, insert heavy-duty metal hollow wall anchors. Push the anchors flush with the tile surface.

③ Apply a bead of silicone caulk around the holes. Position the grab bar, and drive screws into the studs or anchors. Tighten the screws so the bar remains solid when you apply force. Slide the cover plate and snap it over the flange.

Toilet Replacement

A sleek and reliable toilet makes a big improvement over a dingy old-timer that needs its handle jiggled from time to time. For a relatively low cost you can buy a water-saving unit with a modern or more traditional look.

If you have an older toilet, measure from the back wall (not the base molding) to the toilet's hold-down bolts, which are usually covered with ceramic or plastic caps. If the distance is 12 inches, you can buy a standard toilet. If the distance is different (most commonly, 10 inches), look for a toilet to match; it will probably cost more.

Replacing a toilet is easier than you may expect. However, ceramic can crack, so avoid prying hard or hitting it with tools. The main rule: Be sure the water is shut off. If you do not have an individual shutoff valve, you may need to shut off the water to the house.

Environmentally conscious buyers may want to be sure that their toilets are low-water models. Others want confidence in flushing power. Some models now offer two flush settings to have the best of both worlds.

If you're thinking about resale, consider this: A gleaming toilet of a style that harmonizes is certainly not the first thing people look for when shopping for a house, but it will give them a certain peace of mind about the home's general condition.

MATERIALS & TOOLS:

- Toilet, complete with bowl, tank, washers, and the working parts
- Wax ring
- Replacement hold-down bolts, if the old ones are damaged
- Sponge and bucket
- Plumber's putty
- Water supply line, if the old one won't reach
- Hack saw
- Wrenches or adjustable wrench
- Screwdriver
- Penetrating oil

STEP-BY-STEP >>>

❶ **Shut off the water supply** by turning off a shutoff valve just behind the toilet. Flush the toilet, make sure the water is not running, and remove any remaining water with a large sponge. Pry off the caps covering the hold-down bolts, and unscrew the hold-down nuts. If they will not budge, spray with penetrating oil. If that fails, cut through the bolts with a hack saw. Pull the toilet up and out.

❷ **Remove the new toilet bowl** from the box and turn it upside down on a drop cloth or a rug. Press a rope of plumber's putty along the rim of the bowl's base. Fit a wax ring over the outlet opening. Measure to make sure the wax ring is thick enough to amply squish onto the toilet flange on the floor. If not, use a second ring, or extend the flange.

③ Slip the old or new hold-down bolts into the floor flange, and use a bit of plumber's putty to hold them upright. Working with a helper, invert the bowl and carefully set it in place so the bolts slide through the tank's holes. Press down on the bowl with both hands and align it. Slip a washer and nut over each bolt and tighten slowly until the bowl rests solidly. Don't overtighten or you may crack the bowl.

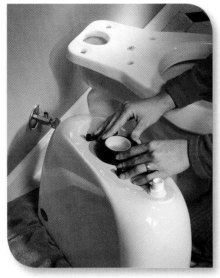

④ Depending on the model of toilet, either place the spud gasket onto the bowl inlet or slip it onto a threaded tailpiece on the bottom of the tank. Be sure the spud gasket has its beveled side facing down.

Flange Extender

If you install new tile onto the bathroom floor, the floor surface may end up more than ½ inch above the floor flange. Adding a second wax ring (see step 2, page 104) may solve the problem, but a better solution is to add a flange extender. Clean the flange, and slip on the extender's flexible gasket and extender ring. Some models have a second gasket that fits on top and takes the place of a wax ring.

⑤ Carefully lower the tank onto the bowl so the spud gasket seats nicely. Slip rubber washers onto the hold-down bolts and slip them through the holes in the tank and in the bowl. Tighten slowly, until the tank feels fairly firm. Do not overtighten.

⑥ Hook up the water supply. You may be able to reuse the supply line from the old toilet. If not, buy a flexible braided supply line made for a toilet, or chrome finished flexible copper tubing, as shown, with compression fittings. Tighten the nuts on both ends, turn on the water, and test. Look carefully for leaks, and tighten nuts if you see any.

TIP: INSTALLING A SEAT

Buy a toilet seat that matches the shape and size of your toilet bowl. To remove a toilet seat, pry up the plastic lids that cover the seat bolts. Hold the nut from below (you may need a wrench), unscrew the bolts from above, and lift out the seat. Clean the area around the bolt holes. Align the new seat with the holes and install the bolts. Tighten the nuts just enough to hold the seat firm.

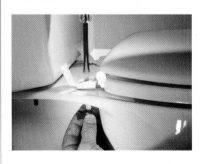

Tub or Shower Surround

Preformed fiberglass or acrylic panels can cover a lot of problems around a tub or shower. At many home centers you can get tub or shower surrounds in a variety of finishes and colors, and with many shelving and soap dish options. Some have a sleek finish, while others are molded to mimic the look of tile.

If your existing plumbing is in good shape and the walls are basically sound, but you don't like the tiles or other wall surface, you can usually tear out the tiles or other surface, do a little general patching, and install the surround on the same day.

In most cases you will want a three-wall surround. Measure your tub or shower base, and order a surround to fit. For a tub, the most common types are made to surround tubs that are 60 inches by 30 or 32 inches. It comes in three pieces, which interlock at the corners for a nearly seamless look.

While you're at it, replace your handles, showerhead, and spout as well. This will give you a total makeover for a modest price.

A molded surround does not have the style of a well-tiled surround, but installing a molded surround is quick and easy. Many people appreciate the modern look and the promise of easy cleaning that these surrounds provide; some people even prefer them to tile.

MATERIALS & TOOLS:
- Three-panel tub or shower surround
- Materials for patching walls
- Cement backerboard if walls behind the surround are damaged
- Adhesive and caulk as recommended by the surround manufacturer
- Drill and hole saw
- Jigsaw
- Tape measure and compass
- Screwdriver and pliers
- Hammer, chisel, pry bar, and other tools to remove existing wall finish

STEP-BY-STEP >>>

❶ **Remove existing tiles or sheets** that cover the surround. The new surround will not extend down to the floor at the front of the tub, so you may need to patch and paint that area.

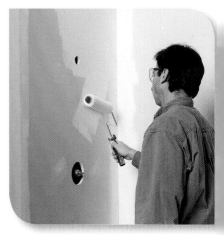

❷ **Patch the walls as needed** for general strength. If the existing wall is crumbling, patch with greenboard or cement backerboard. Prime or seal the walls to ensure the adhesive will stick and to protect from moisture due to condensation. Shut off the water supply and remove the handles, the shower arm and head, and the spout.

③ First install the side panel with the plumbing cutouts. Cut the shipping carton or another large piece of cardboard to make a template the same size as the panel. Measure over from the wall and up from the tub to locate the centers of the handles. Then use a compass to draw circles the size of the openings. Cut the template and test the fit. Make sure the escutcheons and flanges will cover the holes.

④ Lay the first panel on a flat surface that you can drill into. Place the template on top and mark for cutting the holes. Drill small holes using a hole saw. For larger holes, use a jigsaw. Test fit the panel, and trim as needed.

⑤ Use a caulk gun to apply lines of adhesive to the back of the panel. Apply to the middle and to the edges. Set the panel on the tub or shower base, aligned with the back wall, and press it gently into place. Once you are sure of the positioning, press more firmly. Pull the panel back from the wall and wait a few minutes for the adhesive to slightly harden. Press the panel back in place. Run your hand all along the surface until it is firmly attached at all points.

⑥ The remaining panels usually do not need to be cut. Install them in the same way, applying adhesive all along the back surface.

Shower Surrounds

Shower surrounds may come as single units that can just barely fit through the bathroom door, or they may come in separate panels. Many include shower doors, but in some cases you can install a shower curtain instead.

Pedestal Sinks

A pedestal sink has classic appeal; you can choose among styles that harmonize with an old-fashioned or modern bathroom. It takes up less space than a vanity, but does not allow for storage below. Many are surprisingly affordable.

The sink must be supported with a bracket that attaches to strong framing. Unless you already have a wall-hung sink with a bracket mounted at the right height, you will need to cut into the wall, add framing, and patch and paint the wall. Allow several days for this, since you need to apply several coats of patching compound, each of which needs to dry, and then apply paint.

If the pedestal is wide and the supply lines in the wall are closely spaced, you may be able to hide them behind the pedestal. Otherwise, buy good-looking supply tubes and drain parts and let them show.

Bathroom renovations are among the most cost-effective ways to raise a home's appeal and value. A pedestal sink cleans up the look of a bathroom and makes it feel more spacious—and real estate agents will tell you that these are good things. An inexpensive model can recede visually so you can emphasize other bathroom features. A high-end sink can make a great impression.

MATERIALS & TOOLS:

- Pedestal sink
- Bathroom faucet with pop-up assembly and drain body
- Good-looking supply tubes and P trap parts, if they will be visible
- Drywall for patching the wall
- Short 2x8 for supporting the bracket
- Joint compound and drywall tape
- Drywall screws
- Groove-joint pliers
- Drill, hammer, and drywall saw
- Taping blade
- Sanding block
- Paint to match wall
- Primer

A pedestal sink hangs by a wall-mounted bracket; the pedestal itself is more decorative than supportive. The bracket must be screwed to wall framing.

STEP-BY-STEP >>>

1 **Using the dimensions given** in the manufacturer's literature, mark the wall for the bracket location. Cut a hole in the wall that spans between two studs. Cut a piece of 2x8 to fit snugly between the studs, and attach it with screws driven at an angle.

2 **Cut a piece of drywall to fit,** and screw it to the framing piece. Apply joint compound and drywall joint tape to the edges, and smooth with a taping blade. Allow to dry, sand fairly smooth, and apply more compound. Repeat until the area looks and feels smooth, then prime and paint.

3 **Consult the literature again** and drive screws into the 2x8 to install the bracket at the correct height. Set the sink on top of the pedestal and slide the assembly in place to make sure the bracket is at the right height.

4 **Attach the faucet and drain body** to the sink as shown on pages 98–100. Press the sink against the wall above the bracket, and slide it down onto the bracket. Slip the pedestal in to make sure it will fit, then remove the pedestal.

5 **Hook up the drain trap** and the supply lines. See page 99 for instructions on attaching the pop-up assembly. Turn on the water and test to make sure there are no leaks at the supply lines or the drain.

6 **Slide the pedestal under the sink.** Adjust its position as needed so it rests firmly on the floor, is snug against the sink, and looks straight. You may choose to caulk the bottom of the pedestal or leave it uncaulked so you can remove it for cleaning.

Vanity Sinks

A vanity sink has the dual benefit of more surface space and more storage area in the supporting cabinet. Vanity sinks and cabinets are sometimes sold as sets but more often as separate components. A molded vanity top, like the one shown in these steps, includes the sink, counter, and backsplash all in one piece and simply rests on top of the cabinet. For a sink that gets dropped into a separate countertop, see page 112.

Turn off the stop valves under the existing sink and test to be sure the water is off. Disconnect the supply tubes and the P trap, and remove the sink. You may need to repair and paint the wall, unless the new vanity will cover the blemishes.

An attractive vanity that is cleanly installed can be a welcome focal point in a bathroom. Choose a cabinet that fits with the toilet and the tub, a top that harmonizes with the wall colors, and a sink that feels at home with the towel racks.

MATERIALS & TOOLS:

- Vanity cabinet and sink
- Bathroom faucet with pop-up assembly and drain body
- Flexible water supply tubes
- Level
- Measuring tape
- Jigsaw
- Drill
- Caulk gun and caulk
- Stud finder
- Shims

TIP: CHOOSING VANITY COMPONENTS

- Tops made of cultured marble last longer and resist scratches better than most acrylics. Tops made of natural stone are stunning in appearance, but need to be sealed or they may leak.

- A good-quality cabinet is made of solid wood. Inexpensive cabinets made of laminated particleboard are more susceptible to damage by even a small amount of water.

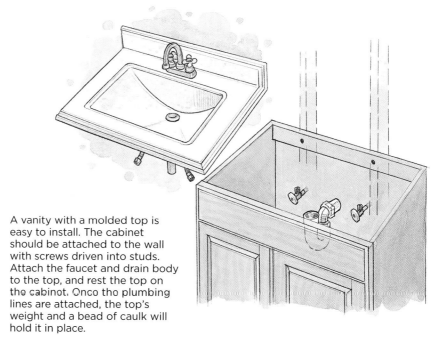

A vanity with a molded top is easy to install. The cabinet should be attached to the wall with screws driven into studs. Attach the faucet and drain body to the top, and rest the top on the cabinet. Once the plumbing lines are attached, the top's weight and a bead of caulk will hold it in place.

STEP-BY-STEP >>>

①Measure to make sure the stop valves and the drain line will fit inside the vanity cabinet. If they need to be moved, hire a professional plumber. If the vanity has a back, remove the handles from the stop valves, then measure and use a jigsaw or a drill to cut holes for the plumbing lines.

②Position the cabinet against the wall, and check for level in both directions. The cabinet doesn't need to be perfectly level, but its bottom should rest evenly on the floor. If necessary, place shims behind the back of the cabinet, and drive screws through the cabinet and into wall studs.

③Install the faucet and the drain body onto the vanity, as shown on pages 98–100. Turn the sink upside down on a stable surface or a pair of sawhorses, and attach the pop-up assembly. Also attach the flexible supply lines and tighten. Test to see that the faucet's lift rod raises and lowers the stopper.

④Place the top onto the cabinet and check that it is centered and tight against the wall. You may want to put some heavy objects like books on it so it doesn't move around while you are connecting the plumbing.

⑤Connect the supply tubes to the stop valves and tighten. Connect the trap and tighten the nuts. With the faucet turned off, open the stop valves and check for leaks. Turn on the faucet and close the sink's stopper to fill the bowl at least halfway. Open the stopper and check for leaks in the trap; tighten nuts as needed.

TIP: CHOOSING SUPPLY TUBES AND TRAP PARTS

- Be sure your flexible supply tubes—which run from the stop valves to the faucet—are long enough to reach. Also be sure that they will fit onto the stop valves; some valves have ⅜-inch openings, and others have ½-inch openings.

- A bathroom sink uses 1¼-inch supply traps. A plastic trap works just as well as a chrome-plated trap and lasts longer, but chrome looks better. Plastic is a good choice for inside a vanity, where it won't be seen.

- You may need to cut trap parts to fit. A hacksaw works fine for either plastic or metal. If you are confused as to how to assemble a trap, or if you have an unusual situation, consult with a plumbing associate at a hardware store or home center.

Drop-In Sinks

A sink that fits into and overlaps a hole cut into a countertop is often called a self-rimming sink. The most common type has a low-profile rim. You can also buy a drop-in sink that rises up to look like a bowl sink.

A drop-in is easy to install once you've installed a countertop with a hole of the right size. At a home center you can find countertops with holes already cut for standard-size drop-ins. Most drop-in sinks have holes for the faucet. If yours does not, you will have to cut them in the countertop.

The photos here show an installation on a laminate countertop. To install a sink into a tiled countertop, see page 78.

MATERIALS & TOOLS:

- Drop-in (self-rimming) sink
- Jigsaw
- Drill with bit ½ inch or longer
- Pencil and tape measure
- Bath caulk or plumber's putty
- Bathroom faucet
- Supply tubes and P trap

STEP-BY-STEP >>>

1 Install a vanity cabinet with a countertop (see pages 110–111). If your sink comes with a paper template, place it on top of the counter, measure to see that the sink will not hit the cabinet below, and trace the outline. If you have no template, place the sink upside down on the top and trace around it; then draw the actual cutout line ¾ inch inside this line. Drill a hole inside the area, then slip the jigsaw blade into the hole and cut along the cutout line. Have a helper support the waste from underneath so it doesn't chip when it falls.

2 Set the sink in the hole to test the fit. Remove it and install the faucet, drain body, and supply tubes (see pages 98–100). Apply a bead of caulk or a rope of plumber's putty around the perimeter of the hole, and set the sink in. If your sink does not have mounting clips (next step), wipe away the excess caulk and wait a few hours for it to set before attaching the plumbing.

3 If your sink has mounting clips, slide them into place and turn them sideways so they grab the underside of the counter. Tighten the screws until the sink's rim is snug against the counter. Attach the supply tubes and the P trap.

Freestanding Bowl Sinks $\boxed{4}$

Some bowl sinks have a sleek modern look, while others are reminiscent of old-fashioned washing bowls. The square sink at right has a wall-mounted faucet that should be installed by a professional plumber. The sink gives the illusion of a bowl with no drain, but actually the P trap and the supply lines are tightly tucked away just below the sink. Again, it is best to call in a professional installer to relocate the plumbing precisely.

If the plumbing parts will be visible, be sure to buy good-looking stop valves, supply tubes, and P trap parts.

Most bowl sinks do not have overflow holes; they have an "umbrella" drain that does not completely close the drain hole.

MATERIALS & TOOLS:

- Bowl sink
- Countertop
- Drill with bits of the right size for the faucet and sink holes
- Faucet
- Drain body and P-trap
- Bath caulk or plumber's putty

STEP-BY-STEP >>>

❶ **Position the sink where you want it,** and mark for the position of the drain hole and the hole for the faucet. Following the countertop manufacturer's instructions, drill holes for the drain and the faucet. Apply caulk or putty around the hole, slip the drain body through the hole, and tighten a nut from below to secure the drain body.

❷ **Set the sink over the drain hole** and screw in the umbrella drain to secure it. Apply caulk or putty around the faucet hole, slip the faucet in (this model has supply tubes already connected), and tighten a nut or screws from below to secure the faucet.

❸ **Connect the supply tubes** to the stop valves and tighten. Cut the trap parts to fit, and attach them. Turn on the water and test for leaks.

CHAPTER 5

You view and greet the world through your home's windows and doors. They frame and showcase the world around you while keeping out unwelcome heat and cold. And these same windows and doors offer opportunities for inexpensive yet often dramatic upgrades for the do-it-yourself homeowner.

Whatever your design style may be, windows play a prominent role. Even if you prefer white walls and unadorned windows, you've established your room's character and mood. Consider these points as you ponder a treatment style:

• Be practical. Window dressings can monitor light, save energy, and ensure privacy.

• Set a mood. Decide on the role your windows should play in a room. Are they an asset worth featuring? Or do they have shortcomings that you can overcome with the right treatment?

• Alter the architecture. Extend window treatments beyond the bounds of small windows to make them look taller or wider. To downplay a window, choose coverings that blend with the wall.

In this chapter we'll look at window treatments, from wispy café curtains to sturdy interior shutters. You'll learn about styles, measurements, and installation techniques. You'll also learn how to install a storm door, adding beauty, energy-efficiency, and air-flow comfort to your home's entryway. And we'll show how to install a new interior door and upgrade the trim around any door in your house for a fresh new look.

Beautifying Windows & Doors

Window Treatments

Windows are often a home's most attractive feature, both for the view and the architectural effect. The vast world of window treatments offers much more than a decorative flourish for your room. Window treatments can also control light, establish mood, preserve privacy, and improve your home's energy efficiency.

In the world of window treatments, hard covering refers to shades and blinds. Pictured below are popular drapery styles:

- Cascading panels bustled to one side add sophistication to the natural formality of double-hung windows.
- Panels on rings capture the sensation of a refreshing breeze with casual flowing ease.
- Dual-fabric panels add flexibility, with sheer panels at ceiling height and opaque panels suspended from a lower rod.
- Full dressing suits homes of elegant, traditional style, often with true transoms.
- Cornice and draperies offer a way to bring a sophisticated window treatment to French doors. The cornice disguises the curtain rod. Be sure the draperies don't impair the door's ability to swing freely.
- Stacking panels are independent overlapping curtains that are relatively easy to install and that offer a popular solution for large window areas.

Cascading Panels

Panels on Rings

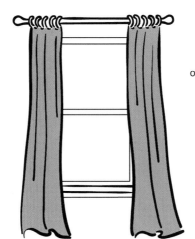

Dual-Fabric Panels

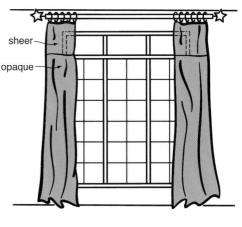

sheer

opaque

Measuring Windows

If you're dressing up several windows, keep a worksheet with measurements and notes for each window indicating the location in the house and the type of treatment. This will be helpful for shopping, ordering, and installation. Pros have a standard system. For instance, in a living room, they label the windows LV1, LV2, etc., starting at the front door (facing the door) and going clockwise around the room.

Once you've compiled an accurate record, keep it on file for the next time you're ready to rethink window treatments. You'll be one step ahead. The method of measuring is straightforward, but it's crucial to be accurate. A retractable metal tape is the most reliable way to measure windows. It's less likely to sag, spans a greater length, and is easier to manage than other methods.

Record a window's measurements in inches, and list the width first, (for example, 30 x 66). For shades and blinds, measure to the nearest ⅛ inch, rounding down for an inside mount.

For best results, measure with a helper, using a metal tape measure. One person measures and calls out the measurement, and the second person writes it down. To check for accuracy, trade places and repeat the process.

Measure a window's width at the top, middle, and bottom. If these measurements vary, use the shortest width for an inside mount and the widest width for an outside mount. If a window is slightly out of square, it will probably not be noticeable. If it is obviously out of square, choose window treatments with an outside mount to mask the problem.

Full Dressing

Cornice & Draperies

Stacking Panels

Drapery Hardware

Rods are still the hardware of choice for supporting most window treatments. The trend is toward thinner rods, but always think in terms of their proportion with the scale of the windows and rooms.

Alternatives to the rod abound, of course. Curtains can be hung from a series of hardware hooks or even strung from a varnished, slender tree limb found in some nearby woods. If it will support your window treatment and appeals to your sense of décor, hang it and give it a try.

Most window treatment hardware is either inside-mounting (installed inside the window casing) or outside-mounting (hung outside the casing on the trim or walls). Either type should be screwed securely into wall studs. If necessary, very light curtains can be supported by wall anchors.

MATERIALS & TOOLS:

- Mounting hardware
- Ladder
- Stud finder
- Wall anchors
- Screwdriver
- Level

Hanging a Curtain Panel

A rod pocket is simply an open hem typically 2 inches wide, just big enough to fit over your curtain rod.

Ribbons add feminine flair. Tie them through half-inch drapery rings inserted in the top hem of a curtain.

Any fabric panel can become a curtain, suspended by these rings and clips, available at fabric stores.

Café

Café rods support simple lightweight curtains. The rods are generally adjustable in length rather than cut to fit. Many have decorative finials and supporting brackets.

Hung at Ceiling

Curtain rods hung at ceiling height draw the eye up and can make the window and the room feel taller. Another trick is to install the rods wider than the window to make the window look larger. These two styles are often combined to enhance a small window.

Hung at Casement

Hanging curtain rods at the top of the casement accents the top of the window. Curtain panels will then cover all four sides of the window, effectively blocking out light when closed without covering the surrounding wall.

Inside Mount

Inside mounting is a good option if window panes are well-recessed from attractive interior trim. Support brackets are screwed directly into the framing under the upper casing.

Outside Mount

Outside mounting has a clean, simple appearance and readily hides unattractive trimwork. Outside mounts can be attached through casings or through the walls outside the trim.

Blinds and Shades

Which of the many styles is right for you? Consider these suggestions:

• Choose woven shades with natural fibers and fabric bindings for a casual look if light control is not a priority.

• Cellular (honeycomb) shades have fabric air pockets that help insulate drafty windows. Many have room-darkening linings.

• Timeless wood blinds offer handsome options—multiple stain and paint finishes, decorative ladder tapes, and shapely valances.

• Shutters present a classic look in painted and stained finishes. Shutters and wood blinds can be made from polymer materials to reduce the warping that may affect wood products in high-moisture rooms.

Installing Blinds

❶ Measure and mark. Usually your shade or blind will snap onto a wand or headrail that is mounted with two brackets (or three for an especially wide window). For an inside mount, as shown, measure 2 inches in from each side jamb and make a pencil mark on the head jamb above the window as shown. Then mark where the screwholes will be by holding each bracket up against the head jamb so it is aligned with the pencil mark. To ensure the bracket is square, line up its front lip with the front edge of the head jamb. With the bracket held firmly in place, mark two screwmounting holes with an awl. Repeat for the other brackets.

❷ Attach the brackets. If you're mounting the brackets on a wood surface, drill pilot holes, then drill in the screws that came with your blind or shade using a 1/16-inch bit.
Tip: If you're attaching to a surface other than wood, you may need to buy wall anchors or toggle bolts; consult the manufacturer's instructions.

❸ Slip the headrail into the brackets per the manufacturer's directions. If your unit also includes a valance, attach it following the manufacturer's instructions. For horizontal blinds, you'll attach a wand for adjusting the vanes. For vertical blinds, you'll first attach the hardware for adjusting the vanes and then slide or snap the vanes into the clips in the headrail.

Woven Shade

Woven shades have a wonderful ability to soften sunlight with their rich textures. They provide privacy with translucency—and can be set at any level you choose. Topped with a tie-up valance, the shade can be raised to disappear when you want to enjoy the full light of the day. Faux-wood blinds—made from polymer substitutes with an appearance similar to wood—resist warming and water spotting, which makes them ideal for kitchens and other high-moisture areas.

Tie-Up Shade

Simple tie-up shades are a creative way to quickly dress up a window. These instructions are for an interior mount shade, but you can install it as an outside mount, as in the photo, by measuring to the outside of your casing.

❶ Measure for an interior mounting. Add a 1-inch seam allowance on the sides and bottom; add 2 inches to the top and bottom. Cut the fabric to these dimensions. Fold over ½ inch on the top and sides. Fold again and stitch hems on sides and top. Fold the bottom of the fabric ½ inch, then 2 inches. Stitch close to the first fold to create the casing.

❷ Cut the mounting board to the desired width. Wrap the top of the fabric around the board and staple the top to the back of the board. Slip the dowel into the casing.

❸ Cut 3-inch strips of fabric to two times the length of the shade plus 4 to 6 inches. Fold over the edges ½ inch twice and stitch to finish. Hem both ends of each piece. Drape fabric strips evenly over the top of the mounting board, in about one-quarter of the width on each side, and staple at the top of the board to hold (Illustration 3).

❹ Use screws to attach the shade from the underside of the mounting board.

MATERIALS & TOOLS:

- Fabric
- 1x2 mounting board
- 1-inch dowel
- Staple gun
- Screwdriver
- Screws
- Needle and thread

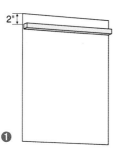

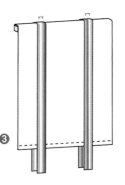

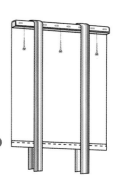

Storm Door

A high-quality storm door correctly installed preserves the finish of your entry door, reduces heat loss, and offers more opportunities for fresh air and sunlight.

Be wary of flimsy, low-cost doors. You'll save money in the long run if you buy a quality door. Look for substantial weatherstripping around the glass panes and the door itself. The frame and hinges should be sturdy enough to stand up to wind gusts. The door frame should be insulated or made of clad wood. The door bottom should have a thick rubber seal that can be adjusted and, when necessary, replaced.

Inspect the opening where the storm door will be installed. The frame and molding should be fairly square and reasonably smooth so the storm door can seal well. At the bottom the sill or threshold should be at an even plane so the door's sweep can seal at all points.

MATERIALS & TOOLS:

- Storm door with latch
- Caulk
- Tape measure
- Drill
- Hammer
- Level
- Tin snips
- Hack saw
- Pliers
- Framing square
- Caulk gun
- Screwdriver
- Nail set

TIP: GET THE RIGHT SIZE

A storm door typically attaches to the exterior framing around your entry door, trimwork called "brick molding." To get a good fit, measure the opening between the side moldings and from the sill to the underside of the top molding. If your doorway is taller than 80 inches, you may need to order a custom-size door. When installing the storm door handle, make sure it won't bump into the handle of your entry door.

STEP-BY-STEP >>>

❶ **Uncrate the door and remove the screen panes** as recommended by the manufacturer. Position the metal drip cap against the top of the entry door's exterior trim ("brick molding") and temporarily attach it with one screw. (These steps may not apply to all doors; follow the manufacturer's instructions.)

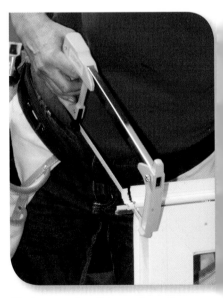

❷ **Measure the distance from the underside** of the drip cap to the sill. Determine which end of the hinge-side Z bar is up. Measure and cut the bottom of the Z bar. If the sill is sloped, make an angled cut that follows the slope.

❸ Set the door in the opening, with the top of the Z bar butted against the end of the drip cap. If needed, adjust the position of the drip cap or trim to the bottom of the Z bar. Temporarily fasten the door with screws at the top and the bottom.

❹ Check for plumb. Test that the door operates smoothly. Adjust as necessary and finish fastening the Z bar. Close the door. Adjust the drip cap so there is a consistent gap of ⅛ inch between it and the door. Drive screws through the remaining holes to attach the drip cap.

❺ Measure and cut the latch-side Z bar. Hold it up against the end of the drip cap and drive two screws to hold it in place. Test the fit of the door and adjust the Z bar's position as needed to achieve a consistent ⅛-inch gap. Drive the rest of the screws.

❻ Close the door and check that it seals snugly against the full length of the weatherstripping. If needed, adjust the positions of the Z bar or the drip cap. Insert the handle parts from each side and drive screws to attach the parts. Attach the latch and adjust so the door closes tightly.

❼ Slip the sweep onto the bottom of the door, and adjust so the sweep's fins touch the sill and compress slightly. Drive screws to secure the sweep.

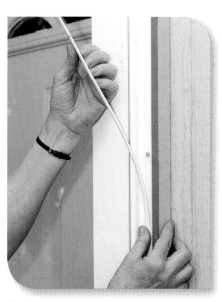

❽ Install the closer and perhaps a wind chain. Some doors come with a cover that fits in a channel to hide the screws. Cut it to length and snap it in place.

Door Casing

Casing, the molding that frames a door or window, covers the gap between the jamb and the wall. These pages show how to install two types of casing, mitered and post-and-lintel. The moldings you choose for either of these types may look different, but the techniques involved will be much the same.

Casings can be cut with a hand miter box and backsaw, though a power miter saw will make the work easier and allow you to slightly adjust angles as needed.

If you plan to paint the molding, you can fill minor imperfections with wood filler or caulk. If you plan to stain, the joints should be as close to perfect as you can get them.

MATERIALS & TOOLS:

- Molding of your choice
- 4d and 8d finish nails
- Hammer and nail set, or power nailer
- Hand or power miter saw
- Tape measure
- Framing square
- Combination square and pencil
- Drill or screwdriver and screws
- Sureform tool or rasp
- Sanding block
- Wood filler and caulk
- Primer and paint or stain

STEP-BY-STEP >>> Mitered Casing

❶ Casings are installed to leave a ⅛- to ¼-inch "reveal" along the jamb. Set a combination square to the reveal of your choice. Hold a pencil against the square's notch and slide the square to draw a straight line all along the head jamb and both side jambs.

❷ Measure from the floor to the head casing reveal line on both sides and cut the casings at 45-degree angles. Position the side casings along the reveal lines and partially drive 4d nails into the jamb and the wall stud. Don't finish driving yet; you may need to make adjustments.

❸ Measure the long distance of the head casing—between the tops of the side casings—and angle-cut both sides. Hold the head casing in position and check for tight fits. You may need to recut. When you are satisfied with the fit, drive nails to fasten. Add a screw as shown. Set the nails and fill the holes.

Post and Lintel Casing

A post-and-lintel casing arrangement calls for no miter cuts, unless (as shown on page 126) you add crown molding at the top. Some designs call for a lintel that overhangs the posts by a half inch or so on each side. In this design, the lintel is the same width as the posts; a thin "parting bead" goes between the post and the lintel and overhangs on either side.

Here we show fluted casing for the sides and a plain 6-inch-wide "frieze board" for the lintel, which may be made of ½-inch medium-density fiberboard (MDF). At the top of the lintel, install narrow crown molding. Plinth blocks are attached at the bottom.

STEP-BY-STEP >>>

❶ Leaving a ¹⁄₁₆-inch reveal at the jamb, drill pilot holes and nail the bottom plinth blocks to the jamb and the wall stud.

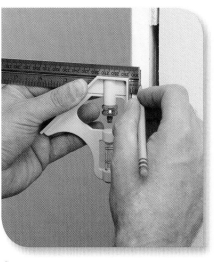

❷ Use a combination square and a pencil to draw a reveal line along the jamb. With this style of casing it is common to have a ³⁄₈-inch reveal.

❸ Rest one end of the casing on top of a plinth block. Using the top reveal mark as a guide, mark the casing for length. Cut with a miter saw.

❹ Rest the cut casing on the plinth block and line it up with the reveal line. Starting at the bottom and working up, partially drive 4d finishing nails into the jamb every 16 inches. Then partially drive 8d nails into a wall stud.

TIP: FLATTEN THE WALL IF IT HAS A HUMP

If a wall has a hump in the middle, your new casing may not lie flat against it. Use a sureform tool, a rasp, or a hand sander to scrape away just enough material to make the wall flat.

Door Casing

(Continued from previous page)

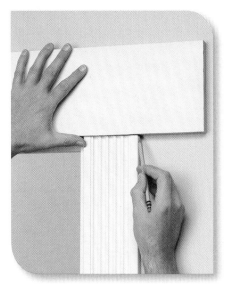

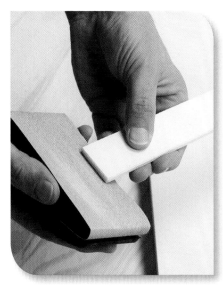

❺ Cut the frieze board to width— 6 inches in this example. Square-cut one end and place it in position on top of the lintel, flush with the edge of one casing. Mark for cutting to length, and cut with a miter saw.

❻ Cut a piece of ¼x1¼-inch lattice or parting stop molding to 1 inch longer than the frieze board. If the molding does not already have a rounded edge, use a sanding block to round it over.

❼ Position the parting bead so it overhangs equally on each side, and fasten it to the top of the frieze board with small brads. The back edge should be flush with the back edge of the frieze board.

❽ Center the lintel (the frieze board with the parting stop) over the posts (the vertical casings). Drive 4d finishing nails into the jamb and 8d finishing nails into the wall where they reach wood framing.

❾ Mark a line ¾ inch down from the top of the frieze board. Cut small crown molding pieces to wrap around (see pages 28-31). You will need to cut two very short pieces to return back into the wall. It may take several attempts before you get this right.

❿ Finish driving nails, and set the heads below the surface. Fill the holes with wood filler. Apply caulk to any gaps, allow to dry, and prime and paint. If you stain instead of paint, do not use caulk.

Pre-Hung Door

I f your old door, jamb, and trim are damaged or just not to your liking, the best solution is to install a pre-hung door. A pre-hung arrives with much of the work done for you: The jamb pieces are already cut and assembled; hinges are perfectly set into mortises in the door edge and jamb; and holes for the door handle and the strike have already been drilled. You might save some money by doing this work yourself, but it would take a lot of time and you would need very good carpentry skills to achieve a professional-looking result.

Some pre-hungs come with the casing molding attached, which is fine as long as you like the casing style. If not, follow the directions on pages 124–126 to install your own.

Start by removing the existing door. Tap the hinge pins up and out, and remove the door. Use a flat pry bar and hammer to remove the casing, then the jamb. If you must pry against the wall, slip a taping knife between the pry bar and the wall so you don't dent the wall.

MATERIALS & TOOLS:

* Pre-hung door to fit your opening
* Door handle (which comes with a strike plate)
* Casing molding
* Wood shims
* 8d and 16d finishing nails
* Tape measure
* Square
* Level
* Drill and screwdriver
* Hammer and nail set
* Hand saw
* Utility knife or hand saw
* Sawhorse

TIP: RIGHT OR LEFT HAND?

Pre-hung doors are sold as either right- or left-handed. Here's how to tell which kind you need: If the hinges are on the left when you pull (not push) the door open, it is a left-handed door. If the hinges are on the right when you pull the door open, it is a right-handed door.

STEP-BY-STEP >>>

❶ **Remove nails** and other obstructions from the opening. Measure the width—from wood stud to wood stud—at several points. Also check the height. Check that the sides are plumb. If not, the opening will effectively be a bit narrower, since you will have to shim it out. Finally, check the thickness of the walls. Most are 4½ inches thick.

❷ **Buy a pre-hung door** to fit the rough opening. The standard doors come in width increments of 2 inches; for example, you can buy units that are 32 inches (2 foot, 8 inches), 34 inches (2 foot, 10 inches), and so on. If your walls are thicker than 4½ inches, you may need to special-order a pre-hung with wider jambs.

Pre-Hung Door

(Continued from previous page)

❸ Some carpenters install pre-hungs with the door still attached, but most find it easier to first remove the door. Tap the hinge pins out, and remove the door. The three jamb pieces will be attached to each other, but not very securely, so take care not to twist them. Also remove the stop molding so you can replace it later to cover nail heads.

❹ Place the jamb set into the opening and check the head (top) jamb for level. If it isn't, shim under the jamb on the low side. Measure the shimmed space, and cut off this amount from the jamb on the other side. To make the cut, place one side piece on the floor and support the other side piece with a sawhorse or table.

❺ Attach the hinge side of the jamb first. If the opening is not plumb, first nail either the top or the bottom (whichever does not need to be shimmed outward). Hold the jamb so it is flush with the wall surfaces on each side. Insert two shims—one from each direction—on the opposite end to make the jamb plumb. Drive two 16d finishing nails just below the shims.

TIP: IF THE STUD IS TWISTED

Studs are sometimes twisted, which means the jamb will be twisted as well, resulting in an uneven opening. Use a carpenter's square to check, positioning the long part of the square along the wall. Drive a shim as needed to bring the jamb square to the wall.

❻ Drive pairs of nails, making sure they go into the wood stud and not the drywall or plaster. Position at least one of them so it will be covered when you replace the door stop (step 10).

❼ Put the door back onto its hinges and tap in the hinge pins. Swing it closed. Halfway between the hinges, insert a pair of shims—one from each side—between the jamb and the stud. Tap in or pull out as needed until the gap between the door and the jamb is equal from top to bottom. Open the door and drive two 16d finishing nails just below the shims.

TIP: RAISING A JAMB FOR NEW FLOORING

Pre-hung doors usually have a 1¼-inch gap at the bottom of the door to allow for clearance over carpeting. If you plan to install new wood flooring or ceramic tiles, shorten the jamb sides by the thickness of the new flooring, plus ⅛ inch (to reduce the gap under the door). If the head jamb is not level, shorten one end as shown in step 5 on page 128. Set the jamb on top of pieces of the future flooring, so you can slip it under the jamb when you install it. (If you plan to install tile, take into account the thickness of the mortar and backerboard.)

⑧ With the door closed, shim and nail the jamb on the strike side as you did for the hinge-side jamb, using three pairs of shims and driving two 16d nails just below the shims. Aim to make the gap between door and jamb perfectly consistent along its length.

⑨ Screw the strike plate to the jamb using the screws provided. Slip the handle's bolt into the door and screw it in place. You may choose to install the handle as well—or do that later, after you've painted or finished the door.

⑩ Close the door so the bolt catches, and hold it snug against the strike plate. Nail the stops. You may be able to simply drive nails through the existing nail holes. If you plan to apply only a coat of finish to the door and jamb, slip a playing card between the door and stop, as shown, to provide the right amount of space.

⑪ Once you are satisfied with the fit of the door inside the jambs and against the stops, drive 8d finishing nails through the jambs and the shims to lock the shims in place. Cut off the shims with a handsaw or utility knife.

⑫ Remove two of the screws from each hinge, and replace them with screws long enough to burrow at least 1 inch into the wood stud. This way, the door will hang from the wall framing, and not just the jamb. Once the door is installed, reattach the casing that came with it, or install custom casing as shown on pages 124-26.

flats

heels

sandals

sneakers

Suede

Canvas & Fabric

Leather

Sole Providers

Extras

There's no doubt about it: We humans love to get organized. Even clutter-prone people like to at least think about putting things neatly in order. The thought of spacious shelves, ample clothes racks, and neatly ordered closets appeals to everyone.

Whether you plan to sell a home soon or to stay forever, it makes good sense to maximize storage space. Home shoppers consistently rank storage high on their wish lists. Little wonder. The average kitchen, for example, needs storage space for nearly 800 items. Kitchen-supply and storage retailers have aisles of solutions. Other solutions are all around you: A shallow pantry can be squeezed into just about any kitchen. Frame the space between two studs, add some shelving and a door. It will swallow up jars and cans. You can create the same space in a bathroom.

Shelving in bedrooms, dens, and family rooms doesn't have to be fancy, especially if it will be filled mostly with books, CDs, and personal treasures. We'll show you how to build basic shelving with a professional appearance. For a living room or entryway, you might want to add dressier shelves; we'll show you how to do that, too.

This chapter also gives plans for closet shelving that makes the most of every square inch, as well as an attractive but easy-to-build window seat with space inside for storing toys or linens.

Finding Storage Solutions

Basic Shelves

Simple, straightforward shelves blend into almost any setting. Here we show building with 1x8 lumber. These shelves are deep enough for most books and memorabilia. If you want deeper shelves, use wider boards or use ¾-inch plywood, which is less likely to warp. Many lumber retailers will rip-cut the plywood to the width you desire.

Start by drawing your shelving plan on graph paper to determine your lumber dimensions. If your shelves will be painted, use inexpensive no. 2 pine lumber or B-grade plywood. If you want to stain the shelves, spend more for a better grade—perhaps "select" or "clear" hardwood or birch plywood.

MATERIALS & TOOLS:

- 1x8 lumber for the shelves
- ¼-inch hardboard or ply for the back
- 1x2 lumber for trim, if desired
- Finish nails and trimhead screws
- Tape measure
- Angle square and carpenter's square
- Circular saw
- Hammer
- Drill
- Wood glue and wood filler
- Sandpaper

STEP-BY-STEP >>>

❶ Cut the sides, top, and bottom. Check one end of each board to be sure it is square; you may need to cut it. Measure over and make a small mark on the board at the correct length. Use your square to draw a cut-off line through the mark. With care you can build clean-looking shelves using a circular saw and a square for a guide.

❷ Using your drawing as a guide, draw square lines on a side piece to indicate the bottoms of the shelves. Place the other side piece alongside the first and extend the bottom cut-off line across the second board. Next to each line, draw an X where the shelf edges will cover it.

❸ On a floor or a large table, set the pieces on edge to form the outer box. Check to be sure each corner is square. Using a drill bit that is slightly smaller than the screws, drill several pilot holes through a top or bottom board and into the side board. Be sure to hold the two boards perfectly aligned as you drill.

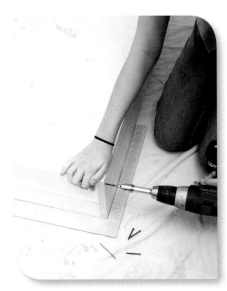

④ Squirt a small amount of glue onto the end of the side piece. Hold the two pieces in position and drive screws until they draw the boards tightly together and their heads sink below the surface.

⑤ Cut the shelves 3 inches shorter than the top and bottom pieces. On the outside of the sides, draw square lines ⅜ inch above the shelf lines from step 2. Fit a shelf in position, aligned with the inside lines, and drive trimhead screws through the outside lines and into the shelf. As you build, check the shelves for square, and measure to make sure they are parallel.

⑥ Cut a piece of hardboard or plywood to the size of the shelf unit, minus ¼ inch in each direction. Place it on the back of the unit, held ⅛ inch back from the edges, and drive small finish nails every 6 inches or so.

⑦ Cover the edges with the trim of your choice. You can get a clean, simple look by placing 1x2 verticals and horizontals flush to the edges of the unit. If shelves are long, attach verticals spaced no farther apart than 3 feet, to make the shelves strong enough to support books. Fill all fastener holes with wood filler, and sand smooth.

Building with Dados

For stronger joints, cut dado grooves in the side pieces and set the shelves into them. To make dado grooves, mark lines for both the top and bottom of the shelf's edge—they will be ¾ inch apart. Set a circular saw to a depth of ¼ inch. Cut to the insides of both lines, then make another cut in the middle. Use a chisel to clean out the area.

Cut the shelves ½ inch longer than the distance between the two outside pieces. Set the shelves into the grooves on one piece, and dry-fit the other side. Make any needed adjustments, then disassemble, apply glue to the grooves, and reassemble. Check for square and drive screws or nails.

Dressed-Up Plain Shelves

Plain shelves don't have to stay that way. You may have—or may even choose to buy—functional shelves that suit your purposes but seem a bit modest in their style. Give them a quick facelift with basic trimwork.

Here we started with three stock cabinets, screwed together. We added a face frame with an arched top piece, side trim pieces, plus stock crown molding at the top and a kick plate underneath. You can play around with the size and configuration to suit your taste, and you may prefer to add more or fewer elements. Experiment with cardboard mock-ups of the trim pieces until you get the size and shape you like.

Your lumber retailer should have appropriate trim boards in a variety of lumber species, and crown molding in multiple styles.

MATERIALS & TOOLS:

- Set of basic shelves
- 1-by lumber as needed for the face and side trim, and for the base
- 2x4 lumber for inside the base
- Crown molding
- Power miter saw
- Jigsaw
- Hammer and nail set or power nailer
- Strip of wood and clamps to mark for a curve (step 1)
- Trimhead screws with drill
- Wood glue and wood filler
- Clamps

Anatomy of a Shelving Facelift

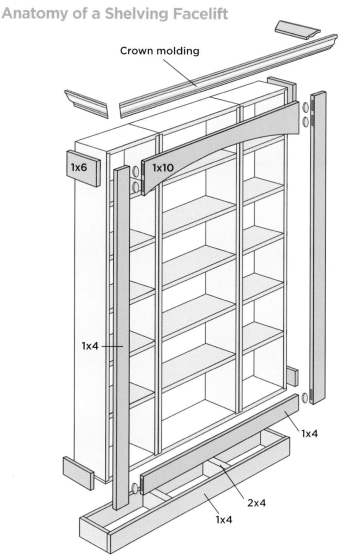

Crown molding

1x6

1x10

1x4

1x4

2x4

1x4

STEP-BY-STEP >>>

① Measure for the length of the top 1x10: the width of the shelf unit, plus the thicknesses of the side pieces, plus ¼ inch. (This will extend the face frame ⅛ inch beyond the bookcase on each side.) Using a narrow strip of molding or other wood, several short boards, and some clamps, make a simple jig arrangement as shown to create a smooth curved line that reaches across the length of the board. When you get the shape you like, trace its outline. Cut the curved line with a jigsaw.

② Build a simple base out of 2x4s and a facing 1x4. To make it recede visually, cut it 2 inches less deep and 4 inches less wide, so it sits 2 inches behind the front of the shelves. You can assemble it with a power nailer as shown, of course—but a screwdriver or a carefully wielded hammer works just fine.

③ Build the face frame. Cut the bottom 1x4 to the same length as the top piece. Set the top and bottom pieces in place and measure for the side pieces. Use wood glue and clamp firmly overnight to attach the pieces. Then screw the face frame securely to the shelves to protect the glued joints.

Using a Biscuit Joiner

If you have a woodworker among your friends, you may enjoy trying out a tool called a biscuit joiner. It helps you make strong joints quickly and accurately by cutting matching slots in boards to be joined. Slim wooden discs—the "biscuits"—are inserted in the slots when the pieces are glued.

You can see biscuits illustrated between the face pieces in the shelving diagram, opposite.

④ Cut the side trim pieces and nail or screw them in place at the top and bottom.

⑤ Follow the instructions on pages 28-31 to cut pieces of crown molding. Fasten them to the bottom of the shelf unit, and fasten them together at the corners. Fill all fastener holes with wood filler, allow the filler to dry, and sand the surface smooth.

Custom Decorative Shelving

A few shelves arranged on a wall can become a focal point for showing off family photos, artwork, flowers, or collectibles. You can buy pre-made shelves, but here we show how to design and install your own.

Size the shelf to suit your needs. It can be as deep as 10 inches, but 8 inches provides enough space for most items.

Start with a straight board, then add molding pieces to the underside and, optionally, the edges. These pages show undergirding a 1x6 board with crown molding, but you can assemble moldings in any configuration that pleases you. For instructions on cutting and installing crown molding, see pages 28-31. For hanging methods, see page 137.

MATERIALS & TOOLS:

- Straight shelving: 1x6, 1x8, or 1x10
- Crown or other molding for under the shelf
- Edge molding
- Wood filler, glue, and sandpaper
- Primer and paint, or stain
- Power miter saw or miter box with backsaw
- Clamps
- Hammer and nail set
- Drill
- Tape measure

STEP-BY-STEP >>>

❶ **Use a power miter saw** or a miter box and backsaw to cut a basic 1-by shelf to length. If you plan to make more than one shelf they can be the same size, which allows you to arrange them symmetrically, or different sizes for a more playful arrangement.

❷ **Cut the molding ends** with 45-degree angles. In most cases, undermounted molding should be an inch or two shorter than the shelf itself. Also cut the short "return" pieces that snug up against the wall.

❸ **Test the fit;** you may need to recut the short pieces. Apply glue to the molding ends that will fit together, and to the top of the molding where it will meet the 1-by shelf.

4 **Use a couple of clamps** to hold the long molding piece in place; test to be sure the short side pieces will fit. Drive finishing nails through the molding and into the 1-by. Apply glue to the short pieces. Drill pilot holes and drive nails to fasten the molding.

5 **Use a hammer and nail set** to drive the nail heads slightly below the surface. Apply wood filler to the resulting holes, and allow to dry. Sand smooth. Apply a coat of primer, then two coats of finish paint. Or apply stain, then a clear finish.

TIP: OTHER LOOKS

You can buy shelves and ornate brackets separately or as an ensemble. The brackets may attach to hidden hardware that mounts to the wall, or you may drive screws through the brackets and into a wall stud, then cover the screw hole with a decorative plug. Sleek modern shelves jut out neatly from the wall and attach using hardware like that shown on the next page.

Installing "Floating" Shelves

A number of common commercial shelves come with hardware similar to that shown here. Installation is simple, but it's important to carefully level the brackets and drive holes in precisely the right spots. If possible, use a stud finder to locate framing behind the drywall, and drive at least some of the screws into studs.

1 **Place brackets atop a level,** or make a level line to use as a guide for bracket placement. Where possible, drive screws directly into studs, or plan to do so after you have attached screws into the anchors. Drill holes for the anchors.

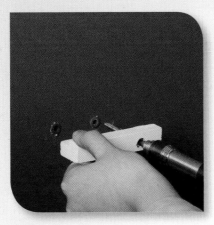

2 **Tap plastic anchors** into the holes. Position the bracket over the anchors, and drive screws to attach.

3 **Slide a shelf over the bracket,** check its side-to-side position, then push down to snap it firmly against the wall.

Off-the-Rack Shelving

There are many ways to hang shelves. These pages show some of the more common methods. Most are simple and easy to install, but keep these points in mind:

- Brackets must be anchored with screws driven into studs. Use toggle bolts or expanding anchors only where the attachment does not need to be strong.
- Use screws that are at least 2 inches long so they extend at least 1½ inches into the wood.
- Take extra care checking that the hardware is precisely level and plumb. You'll notice the difference.
- To make sure the shelves will not sag over time, use the shelving span chart at the bottom of the opposite page to determine how far apart the supports can be.

For ease and versatility, it's hard to beat time-honored vertical standards with brackets to support your shelves. The standards and brackets are thin and unobtrusive visually.

STEP-BY-STEP >>>

❶ **Use a stud finder,** or rap on the wall until you hear a less hollow sound indicating the presence of a stud. Position a standard where you think it's over the stud and poke through with an awl until you can feel the wood behind the drywall. Or drive a small nail to confirm the presence of a stud.

❷ **Determine the desired height** of the standards. Start with the standard at one end of the shelf system. At its top, drive a screw most of the way in. Hold a level against the standard, make sure it's plumb, and use an awl to poke a hole where the bottom screw will go. Drive the bottom hole, check for plumb again, and drive the screws.

❸ **Place a level atop a straightedge** and rest it on top of the first standard. Draw a faint level line. Stand back and see if it looks level in relation to the ceiling; make adjustments as needed. Install the standard on the other end of the shelves as you did the first.

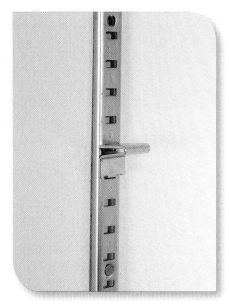

④ Install the intermediate standards. In most homes studs are spaced at 16-inch intervals, so you may not need to test for all the studs.

⑤ Choose brackets long enough to support the width of your shelves. Slip brackets into the slots on the standards. To make sure all the brackets for a shelf are at the same height, count slots up or down from a screw hole.

A different type of standard is used to make shelving inside a cabinet adjustable. Clips are inserted into four standards, two at each end, and the shelves are cut to span from standard to standard.

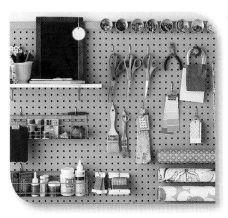

Brackets like these are inexpensive and unobtrusive. Installing them is a bit time-consuming, since you have to measure and fasten each one individually, and they all must be perfectly level with each other.

Use a level and a straightedge to draw a horizontal line that will be covered by the shelf. Use a stud finder to locate framing; every bracket should be attached with screws driven into studs. Faintly mark the centers of the studs just below the horizontal line, where the lines will be covered by brackets. Position each bracket the same distance below the horizontal line, and drive screws deep into the studs to attach the brackets securely.

For a work area, basement, or garage, classic pegboard provides maximum adjustability. Attach 1x2s to studs and attach the pegboard to the 1x2s to provide space behind for the wire brackets.

For adjustable shelving with a more finished look, buy units that have a series of tracks like those shown here. Plastic or metal slips fit snugly onto the tracks, supporting the shelves.

SHELVING SPANS	
Material used	**Maximum span**
3/4" plywood	32"
3/4" MDF or particleboard	24"
1x6 or 1x8 lumber	18"
1x10 or 1x12 lumber	24"

Closet Shelving

Older homes tend to have basic closets featuring a single hanging pole with one or two long shelves above it. This wastes a lot of space and makes non-hanging items difficult to get at, either above or below. Newer closet systems make better use of space and put more things within easy reach.

Home centers and specialty stores have many commercial kits, often made of laminated plywood, that are easy to install. You may want to supplement these with lumber shelves; keep in mind that painting will take more time than installation.

To plan the organization, measure the length and height of your closet. Then measure your clothes and storage items. Group the items according to size to make the most efficient use of space. Measure the horizontal and vertical space needed for each type of clothing; the chart opposite will help. Then make a sketch of your ideal closet, taking into account the ¾-inch thickness of the boards.

Be sure any closet poles are supported every 4 feet or they will sag. Plan to store seldom-used items up high. Avoid tall stacks of clothes, and incorporate storage boxes or bins where possible.

People love closets that make it look easy to keep everything neat and organized. Closet upgrades are a subtle but effective way to improve your home's value.

MATERIALS & TOOLS:

- Shelves, supports, and fastening hardware
- Hanging rods and rod brackets
- Drywall anchors
- Graph paper and pencil
- Hammer and nail set
- Drill
- Stud finder
- Level
- Tape measure and pencil
- Square
- Circular saw or jigsaw

STEP-BY-STEP >>>

① Draw your project on graph paper, including all dimensions. Show your plan to a storage and shelving salesperson, and ask to have some of the parts pre-cut. Usually it is best to leave a few sections uncut so you can hold them in place and cut them precisely later.

② Measure and mark for the shelf supports on the back wall. A standard height is 76 inches for the shelf just above the rod, and 84 inches for another shelf above that. Use a stud finder or tap on the wall and drive exploratory nails (they'll be covered by the shelf support) to find studs. Fasten the supports with nails or screws.

❸ **Assemble a center shelf unit** with shelves spaced evenly or according to your plan. Place the uprights side by side and use a square to mark for the shelf positions. Drive finish nails or trimhead screws to fasten the shelves. Leave the top and bottom open.

❹ **Position the center unit according to your plan,** and mark its location on the floor and on the shelf support. Mark and cut the top of the unit so it is the same height as the top of the bottom shelf support. Then mark for cutting notches so the center unit can go up securely against the wall. Cut with a circular saw or jigsaw.

❺ **Cut the upper shelf** to length and place it on top of the shelf support and the center unit. Drive finish nails or trimhead screws to fasten. Attach the top shelf as well.

❻ **Measure for the locations** of the pole brackets; each should be exactly 3 inches below the shelf. Drive screws to install the brackets on the shelf unit and on the side wall. You probably will not hit a stud on the wall, so use a drywall anchor.

CLOTHING MEASUREMENTS	
Women's	**Length**
Long dress	69"
Robe	52"
Coat	52"
Dress	45"
Skirt or suit	29"
Blouse	28"
Men's	**Length**
Coat	50"
Trousers (cuff hung)	44"
Trousers (double hung)	20"
Suit	38"
Shirt	28"
Tie	27"

TIP: WIRE SHELVING

Wire shelving is inexpensive and easy to clean. Some wire shelves have hanging bars built in. Some retailers will cut pieces to fit your exact measurements. Otherwise, do the cutting yourself with a hacksaw.

Modular Closet Dresser

Looking for a more substantial closet makeover? This one includes drawers and doors that are sold as components. They can be stacked and joined together like building blocks.

The units are more expensive than the shelves shown on pages 140–141, but assembly is actually simple. Once the center section is assembled and installed, wire hanging rods are attached to the walls and to the unit, and that's all the construction. The remaining storage is created with clear plastic bins.

Follow the instructions on page 140 for planning the project to make efficient use of space. In this example, the center section has five components: a narrow three-drawer dresser, a narrow column of shoe shelves, a wider drawer section, a pair of wide shelves, and a cabinet with doors. The manufacturer makes these sections "modular," meaning they can be stacked in various ways and still come out to a uniform width.

These units have maple drawer fronts and doors, but other materials are available. The drawers slide smoothly on high-quality glides.

MATERIALS & TOOLS:

- Modular drawer, door, and open shelf units
- Kickplate unit
- Wire shelves with hanging rods, with brackets
- Screws to tie modular units together and anchor to the wall
- Drill
- Screws
- Tape measure
- Level
- Clamps

STEP-BY-STEP >>>

① Based on your plan, position the kickplate in the center or somewhat off-center in the closet. Allow room for any hanging hardware and storage bins or shelving on each side.

② Join together modular units at the bottom of the system. Here a drawer unit is attached next to a shelf unit (with holes for adjustable shelving, as shown on page 139). Clamp the units together, making sure they are perfectly aligned at the top and along the front. Drill pilot holes and drive four screws to unite them.

③ Position the kickplate and the unit above so their sides are flush. The kickplate should be slightly recessed in the front. Drill pilot holes and drive screws to attach to the kickplate.

④ Continuing to build upward, use the same process to attach other components. Drive enough screws to essentially make the new unit part of the whole dresser.

⑤ Use a stud finder or rap on the wall and drive exploratory finish nails (where they will be covered) to locate studs behind the dresser. Mark the wall above where the top unit will be. To prevent marring the wall, apply painters tape and mark it.

⑥ Attach the top piece to the wall. If its back is recessed so that driving screws would cause it to bend, cut and attach a filler piece to bring the back flush with the top piece.

⑦ Check again that the dresser is positioned according to your plan. Hold a level against it to make sure it is plumb, and press it against the wall. Measure to find where to drive screws into studs; mark on pieces of tape to prevent chipping the wood. Drill pilot holes, remove the tape, and drive screws into studs.

⑧ With the center dresser installed you can insert the drawers. Add hanging rods and shelving to fill in the sides.

CHAPTER 7

Many dramatic electrical improvements can be accomplished by a careful do-it-yourselfer. A change in lighting can add a warm glow or dramatic sparkle that makes any room more inviting.

Most of these projects are quickly installed. Replacing a dull ceiling fixture or installing a dimmer or other specialized switch may take no more than an hour. A hanging pendant light will take a bit more time, and a large section of monorail lighting may involve a half day's work, as will a ceiling fan.

In fact, you will probably spend more time shopping for the right fixture than installing it. You'll be amazed by how well-placed pools of warm light can make your home inviting and user-friendly. Even inexperienced remodelers can easily install simple plug-in puck lights under kitchen cabinets, inside built-in hutches, or in bookcases.

Of course, safety comes first when working with household electricity. Unless you are working with something that simply plugs in (like low-voltage outdoor lights), before beginning work you should *always*:

- Shut off the power at the service panel.
- Test to confirm that the power is off.

Never work in an electrical box that has power present. And if you encounter wiring that you do not understand, call in a professional electrician.

Improving Lighting & Wiring

Ceiling Fixtures

You can dramatically improve the look and feel of a room by installing a new ceiling light. Styles vary, but they all install in one of two ways: either two screws attach the light to a strap in the ceiling box, as shown on these two pages; or a small threaded rod, called a center stud, is threaded through a hole in the center of the fixture, and a nut is tightened onto the stud to fasten the fixture. Most new lights come with an installation strap, stud, or both.

If you don't want to touch up the ceiling paint, be sure the new fixture's canopy—the part that attaches to the ceiling—is at least as wide as the old one. If you'd rather not bother with painting and patching, install a decorative cover called a medallion.

Here we show replacing an existing light fixture that is controlled by a wall switch. If you want to install a new light where there is none now, call in an electrician to run the cables and install the switch and ceiling box. For the two main types of switch wiring, see page 157.

If you have an old ceiling box that doesn't accept the new fastening hardware, take a photo of it to your retailer. Most stores carry hardware for adapting new to old.

A new ceiling light is an improvement that will pay back many times over—as long as the style is right. It's one purchase where a splurge is usually worthwhile. So take your time shopping to find something special.

MATERIALS & TOOLS:
- Voltage tester
- Light fixture
- New strap, if the fixture doesn't have one
- Wire nuts, if they don't come with the fixture
- Electrician's tape
- Screwdriver
- Wire strippers, if needed
- Ladder
- Coat hanger

STEP-BY-STEP >>>

❶ **Shut off the power to the ceiling fixture.** Don't rely simply on the wall switch; in some wiring arrangements (such as switch-loop wiring; see page 155), there will be power present even when the switch is off. So turn on the light, and have a helper watch it as you go to your service panel and flip individual breakers, one by one. Have the helper shout when you've shut off the right breaker and turned off the light. Put tape over the breaker so no one turns it on while you're working.

❷ **Remove the old fixture's globe** and light bulbs. Unscrew the two mounting screws, or remove the nut in the center. Gently pull the canopy down.

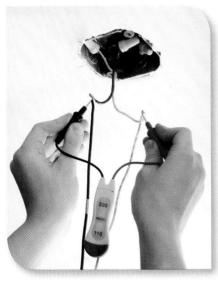

❸ Use a voltage tester to be sure the power is off. Unscrew the wire nuts and touch the probes of the tester to the insulated wires (usually, one black and one white). Also touch the probes to the black (or colored) wires and to the ground wires or to the ceiling box if it is metal. If the tester glows, return to step 1 to turn off the power.

❹ Note how the old fixture is wired, and plan to wire the new one in the same way. Disconnect the wires and remove the old fixture. If the box does not already have a strap with screw holes compatible with your new fixture, install a new strap, or any other mounting hardware supplied with the fixture.

❺ Support the fixture with a bent coat hanger hooked over the strap or ceiling joist to leave your hands free. Connect the fixture's ground wire either to a nut in the box or to a house ground wire. Using plastic wire nuts, splice the fixture's white lead to the house's white wire, and the black lead to the house's black or colored wire.

❻ Carefully tuck the wires up into the ceiling box and push the canopy into position. If the canopy mounts with two screws, start screwing both of them into the strap. Push the canopy tight against the ceiling and tighten the screws. If the fixture mounts with a center stud, thread the stud through a hole in the canopy and tighten a mounting nut.

TIP: CONNECTING WIRES

To splice a stranded fixture lead to a solid house wire, twist the lead around the wire clockwise, allowing about ⅛ inch of the lead to extend past the wire. Push the wires into a wire nut, and twist the nut clockwise until it's tight. Tug on both wires to make sure the connection is firm. Wrap the bottom of the wire nut with electrician's tape.

Ceiling Fixtures

(Continued from previous page)

Installing a Pendant Light

A pendant light hangs from a cable or from a chain through which a neutral-colored cord (which has two wires, plus a ground wire) is threaded. Consult the fixture's installation literature and plan ahead when installing a pendant. In most cases you need to cut the cord or wire and chain to length, then slip on the mounting nut and canopy before attaching the fixture.

Be sure to get the height right. Pendants positioned over a table are often installed about 52 inches from the floor. Without a table, install the fixture so it is comfortably overhead. Experiment with the height before you cut the cord or chain. Check that the light will illuminate well without glaring into people's eyes.

A chandelier is basically a pendant with multiple bulbs and arms. It is installed in the same way but requires the help of a friend to deal with the size and weight.

TIP: MEDALLIONS

If your ceiling is unpainted or damaged in an area too wide to be covered by the fixture's canopy, you may need to patch and paint before installing the light. Or install a medallion to cover the blemishes. Most come with double-sided tape to hold them in place while you install the light. Choose among plain or decorative, and metallic or paintable white.

STEP-BY-STEP >>>

❶ Follow the instructions on pages 146–47 to shut off the power. Test for power, and remove the old fixture. Install a strap that has a threaded center hole. Screw on a center stud (also called a nipple) so it hangs down far enough to mount the canopy. Test to see that the canopy will fit.

❷ If the light has a chain, remove links as needed to hang the light at the desired height. Thread wires up through the chain, and cut them to length so they will fit inside the box. Connect the fixture's ground wire to the house's ground wire or to the box. Strip and splice the wires to the house's wires as shown on page 147—white to white wire and black to black or colored wire.

Track Lighting

Track lighting—now often called monorail lighting—offers a lot of decorative options while also illuminating as wide an area as you choose. This lighting style adds great versatility in distributing light, and the multiple light sources can bring new sparkle to a tired space.

You can run the tracks in different configurations, as shown in the illustration below. And once the tracks are in place, you can install a variety of lamp types anywhere along the track. Some brands allow you to install hanging pendants along with cylinder and bell lamps on the same track.

You can buy a kit that has the track, lamps, and hardware. If you want different styles, or if you want to mix lamp types, be sure that all the lamps will fit onto the track you are using. Usually lamps made by one manufacturer will not fit onto a track made by another manufacturer.

The track you install will carry standard (120-volt) household current. You can attach standard-voltage or low-voltage lamps to the track. Low-voltage lamps are more expensive to buy and will get hotter than standard lamps, but they use less energy.

See pages 146–47 for instructions on shutting off the power, removing an existing fixture, and splicing wires.

MATERIALS & TOOLS:

- Parts for the track system
- Lamps that fit onto the track
- Wire nuts and electrician's tape
- Toggle bolts or plastic anchors, and screws
- Stud finder
- Drill
- Tape measure
- Ladder

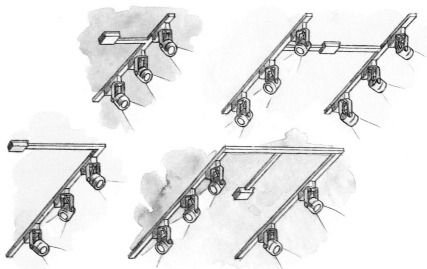

A track system must connect to the ceiling box at some point, but from there you can run tracks in almost any configuration. A track that runs above counters can provide task lighting. Individual lamps may be pointed at artwork or other items you want to highlight. A large system can illuminate an entire room.

Track Lighting

(Continued from previous page)

STEP-BY-STEP >>>

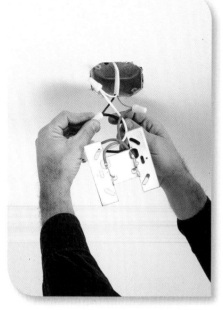 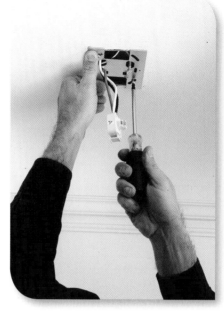 

❶ Shut off the power and test to be sure it is off (see pages 146–147). Remove the existing light fixture. Following the instructions on pages 146–147, connect the mounting plate's ground wire. Splice the white lead to the white house wire and the black lead to the house's black or colored wire.

❷ Push the wires carefully up into the electrical box, push the mounting plate against the ceiling with its holes aligned with the box's mounting holes, and drive screws to attach to the box or to a strap in the box.

❸ Use a stud finder to locate joists in the ceiling, and mark their locations. While a helper holds the other end, position the track on the mounting plate and attach it with screws.

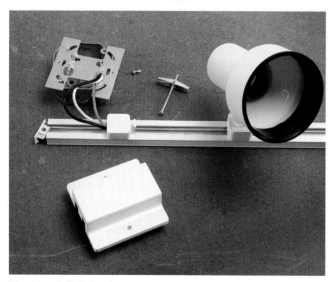

Most track lighting has a mounting plate with wires to connect to a ceiling box. A live-end connector transfers power to metal contact strips in the track. A plastic canopy covers the connections. The track can be mounted using screws driven into joists, or using toggle bolts where there are no joists. Lamps simply twist onto the track; they have metal tabs that contact the electrified strips in the track.

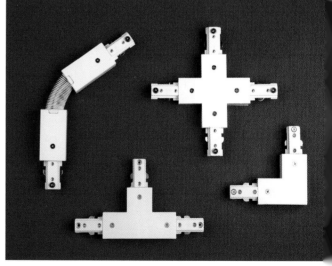

Use a fitting where you want to make a turn or branch out. A flexible fitting allows you to turn at almost any angle. Not al manufacturers have all these fittings. Whenever you install a fitting, be sure to apply an end cap to the other end of the track so it will be energized.

4 **Measure out from the wall** or a cabinet to position the track parallel to the wall, or in the alignment you choose.

5 **If the track runs across joists,** drive mounting screws through the track and into the joists. If the track runs parallel to joists, drill holes about a foot apart. Tap plastic anchors into the holes, then drive screws into the anchors. For a stronger connection, use toggle bolts.

6 **To turn a corner or branch off** in a T, snap the fitting onto the end of the track you installed. While a helper holds the other end of the new track, slide it onto the fitting. Attach the new track as you did the first. Cover all open ends with caps.

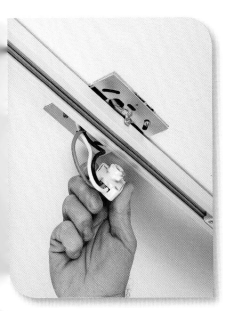

7 **At the mounting plate,** push the live-end connector into the track and twist it so it seats snugly. Snap the canopy over the connector.

8 **Some lamps simply twist onto the track.** (You may need to depress a tab in order to untwist them for moving.) Position the lights where desired. Restore power and test. If a lamp does not work, you may need to twist it a bit more firmly. Rotate the lights to achieve an effect you like.

Ceiling Fans

A ceiling fan's gentle movement of air reduces the need for air conditioning, potentially saving energy costs.

Choose a fan scaled to your room. Install a 42-inch fan in a room that is 12x12 or smaller, and a 52-inch fan in a larger room. For a fan to effectively circulate air, its blades must be at least 10 inches from the ceiling.

If you want the ceiling fan to have a light, many are sold with a light kit included; other manufacturers sell the light kits separately.

Keep in mind that ceiling fans are heavy and they vibrate. They require firm support. Unless one is already in place, you will need to install a fan-rated ceiling box, or mount the fan's bracket on a nearby joist.

Many ceiling fans have small canopies, the cover that fits against the ceiling. Your new fan may not conceal the unpainted ceiling area left when you remove the old fixture. Plan to patch and paint or buy a medallion.

MATERIALS & TOOLS:
- Fan-rated ceiling box or hardware suited to your situation
- Ceiling fan
- Light kit, if desired and not included with the fan
- Screwdriver
- Voltage tester
- Hammer and flat pry bar
- Keyhole saw or reciprocating saw (if necessary)
- Drill
- Wire strippers
- Ladder

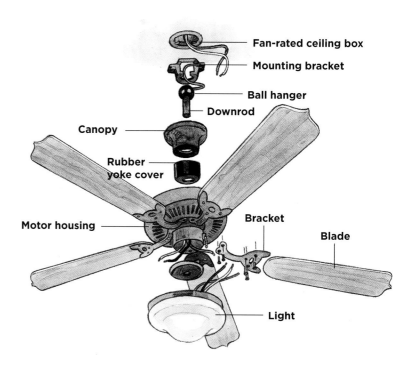

Fan-rated ceiling box
Mounting bracket
Ball hanger
Downrod
Canopy
Rubber yoke cover
Motor housing
Bracket
Blade
Light

Removing an Old Box

Boxes are attached in various ways. If yours is simply nailed to the side of a joist, first insert a short piece of wood into the box, and tap it upward. Then use a flat pry bar to pry it away from the joist.

If prying doesn't work, try cutting through the nails. This is easiest to do using a reciprocating saw, but you can also use a keyhole saw with a metal-cutting blade. You may need to cut the ceiling drywall to access the nails. Shine a flashlight up into the opening to locate the electrical cable, and take care not to cut into the cable.

An old pancake box may be mounted with screws driven into a joist. Remove the screws, pry the box out, and pull the box down.

Installing a New Box

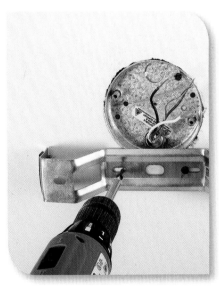

Remove the cable from the old box. Cables attach to boxes in various ways. You may need to unscrew a cable clamp or a set screw. Or, in the case of a plastic box, as shown, you can simply poke a tab to free the cable.

At a home center you will find fan-rated boxes to suit most situations. The boxes shown here attach directly to the underside of a joist. If your box is located between joists, install a brace and box as shown on page 154.

If there is a nearby joist, you can follow another strategy altogether: Instead of removing the box, position the fan's mounting bracket (see page 154, step 1) alongside the box. Drive screws through the bracket and into the joist to firmly attach it.

Ceiling Fans

(Continued from previous page)

STEP-BY-STEP >>> Installing the Fan

① **If a joist runs through the middle** of the hole, simply fasten the box with two or three wood screws (not drywall screws, which are not strong).

② **Once you have run cable** into the box and installed it, attach the fan's mounting bracket. Drive the screws provided into the fan-rated screw holes. If there are rubber washers, install them between the bracket and the box.

③ **Thread the wires through the canopy** and the downrod. This fan also has a yoke canopy between the canopy and the fan. Attach the downrod to the fan with a hanger pin and a retaining clip. You may need to cut and strip wires (see page 146) so they won't be too long and crowd the box.

Installing a Box with a Brace

① **If you have access** to an unfinished ceiling above, it is probably easiest to work from there. Move aside any insulation to expose the old box. Carefully remove it, and install a new braced box as shown.

② **If you must work from below** and the hole is between joists, buy a braced box made for remodel work. Slip the brace through the hole and turn it so its legs rest on top of the ceiling drywall, perpendicular to the joists. Rotate the shaft of the brace clockwise until it snugs against a joist on each side.

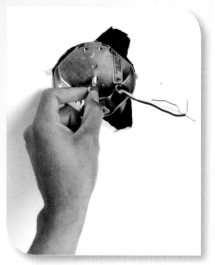

③ **Use a pair of pliers** or a crescent wrench to firmly tighten the brace. Run the cable into the box and clamp it firmly, following the manufacturer's instructions. Attach a U-bolt to the brace and slide the box up through it. Tighten the nuts.

4 Lift the assembled fan and hook the downrod's ball-like end to the mounting bracket. This will hold the fan in place while you do the wiring.

5 Wire the fan, following the manufacturer's instructions. See page 156 for different wiring arrangements; you may want to install a remote-control receiver. Often, the black lead controls the motor and the blue or striped lead controls the light. If you have only a black and a white wire (in addition to a ground), splice both the motor and the light wires to the black wire. Make all connections firmly using wire nuts (see page 147).

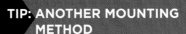

TIP: ANOTHER MOUNTING METHOD

Some fans, like the one shown here, have a mounting bracket that looks more like a plate that fastens up against the ceiling. The downrod has a hook that hangs onto a metal loop in the mounting bracket to hold the fan in place while you wire it. After wiring, slide the canopy up and attach it to the bracket using side screws; the ball in the downrod rests snugly in the canopy, which actually supports the fan.

5 Carefully tuck the wires up into the box. Push the canopy up against the ceiling and fasten it with one or more setscrews. Screw a fan bracket onto each fan blade. Attach the fan brackets to the underside of the motor. Make sure all screws are tightly fastened.

6 Remove the cover plate on the bottom of the fan and wire the light kit. The fan shown here has plug-together connections; other fans require wires to be spliced with wire nuts.

7 Fold the wires into the housing and push the light kit onto the fan. Tighten the screws to secure it. Install any lightbulbs and the globe.

Ceiling Fans

(Continued from previous page)

Switch and Wiring Options

If you are replacing a ceiling light, you probably have two or three wires (a white neutral wire plus a black or colored hot wire, and possibly a green or bare ground wire) running from the switch to the light. In this case, you can choose among the first three options shown on this page. If you have three-wire cable (a white, a black, and a red or other colored wire) along with a ground), you can wire using option number 4. See "Ways to Wire a Switch," opposite, for the most common ways light switches are wired.

TIP: FAN-ONLY SWITCH

If you install a fan with no light, you could simply wire a switch for it as shown opposite and control the fan's speed levels using the pull chain. Or install a switch like the one shown below, which operates the fan at different speeds.

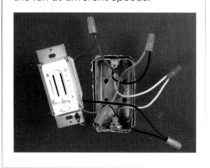

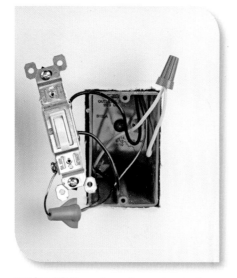

Option #1: If you have two wires in the box, you can continue to use the existing switch, or hook up a standard switch as you would for a regular ceiling light: attach the black wire to the brass terminal, the white wire to the silver terminal, and the ground wire to the ground terminal. Install the fan with two pull chain switches. Use the wall switch to turn on the unit, and use the pull chains to control the light and the fan separately.

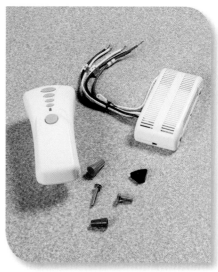

Option #2: Buy a remote-control switch and sending unit made specifically for a ceiling fan, like the one shown. Following the manufacturer's directions, install the switch's sending unit inside the fan's canopy; wiring for the fan and the light will be connected to it. You can now control the fan and the light separately using a remote-control switch, which may be hand-held or mounted to a wall so it feels like a regular switch.

Option #3: Spend a bit more for a ceiling fan that includes its own switch that controls the fan and the light separately. Wire the switch as you would a dimmer (see next page).

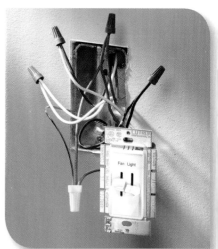

Option #4: If you have three-wire cable running from the switch box to the ceiling box, install a fan/light switch like the one shown. Splice the switch's black lead to the black wire bringing in power. Splice all the white wires together. Splice the switch's light lead to the wire running to the light, and the switch's fan lead to the wire running to the fan.

Switches

A dimmer switch lets you set just the right mood, and it makes a room feel a bit more elegant. Other special switches shown on the following pages give you even more control. Installing these switches is simple, as long as you take care to work with the power shut off.

Special switches make a house feel a bit special, and are usually well worthwhile—especially since most of them cost less than $20 and install in less than an hour. In addition to special switches, you may want to consider color and style options for switches. Rocker and "decora" switches, for example, have an upscale feel.

In most cases you can simply replace a standard switch with a dimmer of any style. However, there are exceptions:

- Do not use a regular dimmer to control a fan or a fluorescent light. Many will burn out. Instead, purchase a dimmer specially made for a fan or a fluorescent.
- If a light is controlled by two different switches, it is a "three-way" configuration. Buy a special dimmer made for three-ways.
- A dimmer will not work for low-voltage halogen lights.
- Most dimmer switches are rated at 600 watts, which is plenty for most light fixtures. However, if you have a large chandelier with bulbs that total over 600 watts, buy a switch with a higher rating.

Ways to Wire a Switch

As a general rule, you should wire a new switch in the same way as the old one; if you see a configuration that you do not understand or that doesn't line up with your new switch, take a photo and consult with a wiring expert at a home center or hardware store, or ask an electrician.

When you open a box, you may find one or two cables, each with two or three wires plus a ground wire, entering the box. If power enters the switch box and then goes on to the light box, you'll see two cables (see below). This is called "through-switch" wiring. The white wires are spliced together, and the two black wires attach to the switch's two terminals or leads. If power runs first to the light's box, the arrangement is called "switch-loop" or "end-line" wiring. Only one cable enters the box.

Both the black wire and the white wire (which should be marked black, but often isn't) connect to the terminals or leads.

If two switches control one light, that's called a "three-way" wiring configuration. A three-way switch has three terminals (plus the ground terminal), and its toggle doesn't have On and Off markings. It must be replaced with a new switch that is also three-way. Three-way wiring can get complicated. Before you disconnect the wires, use a piece of tape to mark the wire that attaches to the darker-colored "common" terminal, and attach it to the common terminal or lead on the new three-way switch. The other two wires can attach to either of the two "traveler" terminals.

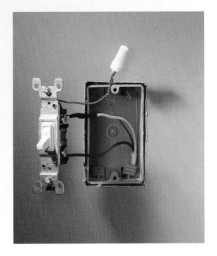

Special Switches

Timer

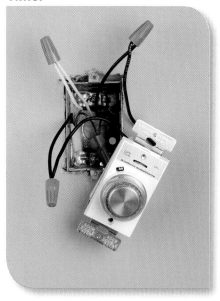

A simple timer switch turns lights on and off once a day. It is most often used to turn outdoor lights on at night and off in the morning.

Programmable

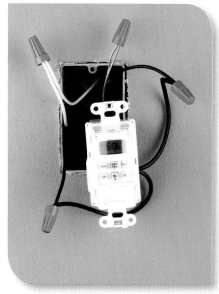

A programmable switch can turn a light on and off more than once per day. This could, for instance, fool potential robbers into thinking someone is at home while you are away on vacation.

Time-Delay

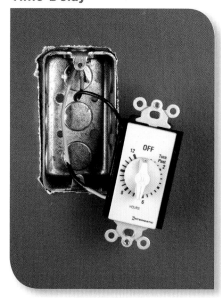

A time-delay switch turns a fixture off after a designated time interval. These are popular on vent fans, heat lamps, and other devices that you don't want to monitor and turn off manually.

TIP: MAKE SURE IT WILL WORK FOR YOU

Read the label on a switch carefully and consult with an electrical salesperson to make sure it will work in your situation.

• Some switches can be installed only if you have through-switch wiring, with two cables entering the box; they cannot be installed with switch-loop wiring (see page 157).

• If you are replacing a three-way switch (see page 157), be sure to replace it with another three-way switch.

Pilot Light

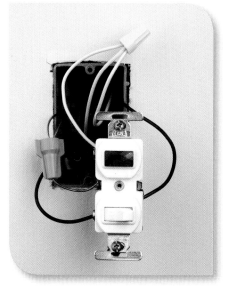

This light has a small bulb that glows when the light or fan is on. Use it, for instance, to control a garage or shed light that you cannot see from inside the house, so you won't inadvertently leave it on all night.

Motion-Sensor

This switch turns on a light when it senses movement in the room, then turns it off after a set amount of time. Some models allow you to adjust for sensitivity and to determine how long the light will stay on. It's often used for outdoor lights, to repel intruders and light the path to the door.

STEP-BY-STEP >>> Installing a Dimmer or Special Switch

A dimmer switch is a rheostat, a device that controls the amount of current that reaches a fixture. Some new kinds of bulbs require specialized dimmers, and some simply won't work with dimmer switches, so check with your retailer to be sure you're buying a switch that will work with your fixture. Apart from that, specialty switches are a fun category for the do-it-yourselfer. The process is simple, the cost is minimal, and the result can be quite dramatic. Just be absolutely certain that the circuit has no power while you're working, and note carefully how the wires were connected to the switch you're replacing. This work doesn't involve many steps, so take your time with each one.

MATERIALS & TOOLS:

- Dimmer or other special switch
- Wire nuts (which usually come with the switch)
- Voltage tester
- Wire strippers (or side cutters or lineman's pliers)
- Screwdriver
- Small level

❶ **Turn on the light,** and go to the service panel to shut off the breaker (see page 146); doing so will turn the light off. Remove the screw holding the cover plate and remove the plate. Touch the probes of a voltage tester to the switch's two terminals and to the bare wires attached to the terminals; the tester's light should not glow.

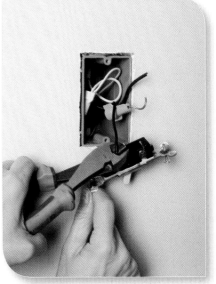

❷ **Once the power is off,** unscrew the mounting screws and carefully pull the switch out. You could loosen the screws holding the wires, but it's better to cut and restrip the wires, since they've been bent and might be about to crack. Use a pair of side cutters, lineman's pliers, or the cutter on a pair of wire strippers to clip the wires at the switch.

❸ **Strip about ¾ inch of insulation** from the wire ends. Slip the wire into the correct hole of the strippers (usually #14), squeeze, twist slightly, and pull the insulation off. If you nick the bare wire deeply, clip and try again with a larger hole.

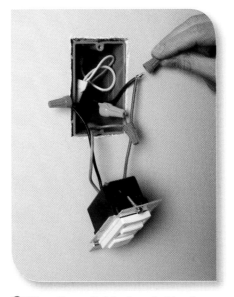

❹ **Wrap the switch's stranded lead** clockwise around the bare house wire, allowing the stranded lead to extend about ⅛ inch past the wire. Twist on a wire nut and tighten. Tug on both the wire and the lead to make sure the connection is firm. Also attach the ground lead (which is green or bare) to the house's ground wire or to the box.

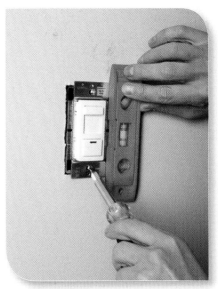

❺ **Carefully fold the wires** back into the box. Push the switch into position and attach with the hold-down screws driven into the holes in the box. Use a small level to check that the switch is plumb, then fully tighten the hold-down screws. Mount the cover plate. Restore the power and test.

CHAPTER 8

People who are drawn to the backyard to lounge, garden, dine, and socialize are the happier for it. Casual structures can provide the bait. If you don't have the funds to pay a landscaper to build a major project, no worries; many inexpensive projects completed by homeowners are every bit as charming and useful as those made by the pros.

More and more, folks think in terms of "outdoor rooms"— defined areas devoted to cooking, eating, and relaxing. A patio floor clearly defines a room. Trellises, arbors, and lights can also casually frame sections of a yard.

When you're outdoors, decorating decisions are often easier than they are for indoor projects—especially if you use natural materials, which almost always look great next to each other, and next to foliage. The projects in this chapter emphasize natural materials such as wall stone, ceramic tile, wood for arbors, and flagstones. One project uses stackable concrete blocks, but you can find styles that mimic the look of real stone.

Many projects, such as stone walls and patio surfaces, can be scaled to fit your goals and budget. This book's promise of upgrades "under $600" would dictate a short decorative wall or a modest patio area. But the techniques and steps described in these pages will ensure your success on projects large or small.

Adding Yard Improvements

Flagstone Patios and Paths

A beautiful natural flagstone patio complements any outdoor style. The method shown here is the simplest installation: Set the stones in a bed of soil or sand. It's likely you will need to remove and reset some stones every few years, especially if there are nearby trees with large growing roots. For a more ambitious flagstone patio installation, see pages 166–177.

This method also allows "crevice" plants to grow between the stones. Plan for the plantings; some plants do well with a sandy soil. If the plants you prefer grow best in unsandy dirt, either set the flagstones in soil only or dig away the sand in the joints before planting.

The term "flagstone" refers to any rough, uncut stone that is fairly flat and between 1½ and 3 inches thick. If the flagstones are milestone, they will be strong enough for a soil-laid installation as long as they are at least 1½ inches thick. Sandstone or slate flagstones need to be thicker or they may crack. (To install thinner stones, set them in mortar on a concrete slab, as shown on pages 170–171.)

A well-laid and well-maintained flagstone patio will certainly raise a home's value, so take time to arrange the stones with joints that are fairly consistent in width, and work to maintain a level surface. As a final touch, attractive crevice plants can transform a plain patio into a sumptuous garden floor.

MATERIALS & TOOLS:

- Flagstones
- Bedding sand, also called torpedo sand
- Sod cutter
- Shovel (spade) and garden rake
- Hand tamper or rented power tamper
- Brickset chisel and hammer or mallet
- 4-foot length of straight 2x4
- Garden hose
- Heavy broom

STEP-BY-STEP >>>

❶ **Lay out the patio area.** A flagstone patio usually looks best with curved rather than straight lines. "Charge" a hose by closing the nozzle and filling with water, to make it a bit firmer. Use the hose to create the shape of your future patio. Pour sand along the hose's length, and remove the hose to reveal a clear perimeter line.

❷ **Use a shovel or sod cutter** to remove sod. Also cut away roots thicker than ¼ inch. Dig to a depth equal to the thickness of the stones—plus 1 inch for the sand, if you will use sand. If the soil is very hard, consider renting a rototiller. Rake the soil, then tamp down with a hand tamper or a rented power tamper. Pour sand into the area, rake fairly smooth, and tamp.

❸ Working from the perimeter toward the center, lay large stones first. Aim to create joints that are fairly consistent in width. Cut stones as needed (see below). If a stone juts out beyond the excavated area, cut away the sod rather than cutting the stone.

❹ Use a straight board to check that the surface is reasonably even. If a stone is too high or low, remove it and either dig away or add sand below. Work slowly, taking breaks to relieve strain on your back. Stand on the stones to check for rocking, and adjust the subsurface to achieve stability.

❺ Fill the joints with soil. If desired, sow seeds for low-growing crevice plants, or insert small plants. To plant moss, mix the moss of your choice with equal parts buttermilk and soil, and pour or slather over the joints. Allow to dry, and sweep the stones clean. Spray with a fine mist and add soil as needed.

Cutting Stones

Use uncut stones wherever possible, but you will need to cut some stones. To mark for cutting, lay the stone over an adjacent stone and trace the outline with a thick pencil or a piece of chalk. Place the stone on a stable surface (a sand bed is good) and pound along the line with a hammer and brickset chisel to create a line at least ¼ inch deep. Position the stone with a scrap piece of wood under the cut line. Have a helper stand on the stone, place a piece of plywood over the area to be cut away, and smack it with a small sledgehammer to complete the cut. Or cut along the line using a grinder equipped with a masonry blade. Wear protective clothing and eyewear. Cut partway through, then break it off. Tap along the cut edge with a hammer to create a natural-looking perimeter.

Flagstone Patios and Paths

(Continued from previous page)

Other Patio Options

A very stable stone patio is set on sand over a bed of gravel, s shown in the illustration below. Excavate to a depth of 10 inches or so (depending on the thickness of the stones) and use a rented vibrating compacter to tamp the soil firmly.

Spread a 4- to 6-inch layer of compactible gravel (also known as aggregate base or hardcore) and tamp it as well. If you don't want plants to grow through the joints, lay sheets of landscaping fabric over the gravel. Set your edging to secure the landscaping

fabric. Then add a 2-inch layer of sand, and set the stones.

In areas with lush vegetation, the landscaping fabric may be less effective. An extra inch of sand can help reduce the nuisance of unwanted vegetation.

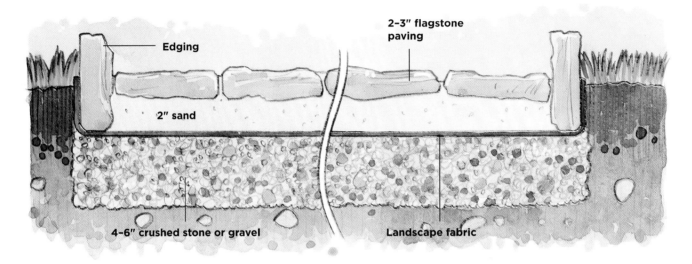

Edging

2-3" flagstone paving

2" sand

4-6" crushed stone or gravel

Landscape fabric

In some areas of the country you can buy very large sandstones for paving. Installing these is a job for a small crew—at least three people. The base must be carefully prepared so the stones are supported at all points to avoid cracking. Smooth the sand, set a stone, then pick it up again. Examine the back of the stone and the sand bed for indentations and gaps that show where the stone is unsupported, and fill as needed. You may need to spray the sand with a fine mist in order to see the patterns. You'll probably need to repeat these steps several times in order to achieve stability and full support.

TIP: EDGINGS

Large, heavy stones will stay put when walked on, but smaller stones may need to be enclosed. Planting sod right up to the edges can help keep them in place, but for more serious enclosing you may choose to add edging.

To install timber edging, cut 4x4s, 6x6s, or railroad ties to length. Lay the gravel base but not the sand, and set the timbers on the gravel. Drill holes every 3 feet or so and drive 2-foot-long pieces of metal reinforcing bar (rebar) down through the holes and into the soil.

Plastic "hidden" edging is barely visible once the grass is replanted. Install it while you lay the stones, driving stakes to hold it in place.

Crevice Plants

A home center or nursery may sell plants that work well in the crevices between flagstones. They may be called "steppers" because they can endure at least light foot traffic. Consult with a plant expert to choose crevice plants that will thrive in your situation. Factors to consider include sun, amount of rain, how well drained the soil is, and how often the plants will be stepped on. You may opt for several different types; after a year you may find that some work better than others.

Flagstone Path

A curving flagstone path usually looks better than a straight one, because the stones are irregular to begin with. If you need to make a straight path, consider timber edging, as shown on the previous page.

STEP-BY-STEP >>>

❶ To maintain a reasonably consistent width, cut boards to the same length. Set out hoses and lay the boards between them every 2 feet or so. Pour sand or flour over the hoses and remove the hoses to reveal clear lines.

❷ Cut away the sod and excavate. Remove any roots over ½ inch in diameter. Simply excavate an inch below the bottom of the stones, or dig deeper if you will install a gravel bed, as shown on the previous page. Use a vibrating plate compactor to tamp the soil, then the gravel (if any), then the sand. You may choose to install plastic hidden edging.

❸ Arrange the stones carefully, and stand back every 15 minutes or so to appraise the pattern and give your back a rest. Wherever possible, install larger stones on the perimeter. You don't need the stones to reach all the way to the grass on either side; you can fill in the edges with sod later.

❹ Test the stones for stability, and remove and adjust the sand base as needed. Spread sand over the surface and use a broom to clean the stones and fill the joints.

Tile on Concrete

If you have a concrete patio that's unattractive but solid, tiling over it can transform it from an eyesore to an inviting outdoor floor.

First, examine the concrete. If there are large cracks and sections that are more than ½ inch above or below an adjoining section, the slab is probably unstable and will continue to deflect. Tiles will not fix that problem, so consult with a concrete professional to see if it can be repaired or if you need a new concrete slab. Minor problems can be solved using the techniques shown on these two pages.

Choose tiles guaranteed to survive in your climate. There are plenty to choose from, including glazed or unglazed ceramic tiles, quarry tiles, porcelain, stone, and terra-cotta. Mexican saltillos are popular in warm climates but can crack in freezing weather. Unglazed tiles make for a less slippery surface when it rains. Use sanded grout that is fortified with latex, polymer, or epoxy. If the tiles are regularly shaped and the joints are not too wide, use plastic spacers to maintain straight and consistent grout lines.

Many potential buyers love the idea of spending time outdoors, and an attractive patio can be a strong selling point.

MATERIALS & TOOLS:

- Self-leveling compound, patching compound, and isolation membrane as needed
- Hammer or hand sledge and cold masonry chisel
- Concrete bonding liquid
- Grinder with masonry wheel
- Outdoor-rated tiles
- Plastic spacers
- Sanded and reinforced grout
- Thinset mortar
- Wet-cutting masonry saw (rented)
- Tape measure and chalk line
- Level or straightedge board and pencil
- Notched trowel (with notches the size recommended for your tiles)
- Foam backer rod
- Exterior caulk
- Five-gallon bucket and drill with mixing paddle
- Grout float and sponge
- Grout bag for wide joints
- Shop-type wet-or-dry vacuum

STEP-BY-STEP >>>

❶ **Use a 4-foot level** or straightedge board to check the slab for evenness. Mark any low or high spots with a pencil. Minor low spots and holes can be filled when you apply the thinset, but even the smallest high spots must be removed.

❷ **To fill a depression,** mix self-leveling compound or thinset mortar and pour it onto the area. Use a straight board to smooth out a large area, or a trowel for a smaller area. Finish with a trowel, feathering the edges and taking care not to create high spots.

③ **Use a right-angle grinder** equipped with a masonry wheel to grind away high spots. Wear protective clothing and eyewear, and hold a vacuum near the grinder to collect dust. Damp-mop the area thoroughly.

④ **Use a hand sledge** and a cold chisel to widen small cracks so you can fill them. Brush out any debris, then vacuum. Dampen and wipe or brush the inside of the crack.

⑤ **Coat the inside of the crack** with concrete bonding liquid. Fill the crack with patching cement or thinset mortar. Feather it out so there are no high spots. Cover the surface with an isolation membrane, which reduces the risk of tile damage if the concrete shifts.

STEP-BY-STEP >>> Setting Tiles

⑥ **If the edge is damaged,** chip away any loose concrete, clean, and patch.

① **Follow the instructions** on pages 48–49 to plan the layout. Use either measurements or a dry run with spacers to make sure you will not end up with a narrow row of tiles along any edge. Draw or snap layout lines. Use a drill with a mixing paddle to mix a batch of thinset mortar and apply with a notched trowel. Work in areas about 4 feet square—smaller if conditions are hot and dry—so the mortar does not start to harden before you finish setting tiles. Set tiles in the thinset and give them a slight twist and a push to bed them. Use plastic spacers to maintain even gaps between tiles.

② **Lift up a tile** every so often and inspect its back side. If less than 75 percent is covered with mortar, either apply a thicker coat of mortar, or back-butter the tiles. If a tile is too low, pick it up and apply more mortar.

TIP: CLEANING AND BONDING

If there is any oil or tar on the concrete surface, the thinset—and the tiles—may not stick. Clean the entire slab with detergent, or pressure-wash it. For more assurance of stickability, pour concrete bonding liquid and spread it with a broom.

Tile on Concrete

(Continued from previous page)

❽ **After you've finished a section,** clean out mortar that is less than ¼ inch from the tile surface. Plastic spacers work well for this.

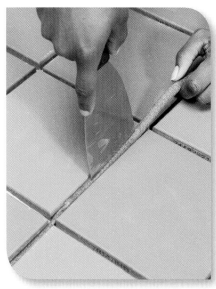

❹ **If the patio is longer** than 8 feet in any direction, insert a foam backer rod in the middle of the area, to protect against cracking due to changes in temperature. Apply silicone caulk above the backer rod and allow it to dry before you start grouting.

❺ **To mark a tile for cutting,** set the tile to be cut on top of the last set tile, with the edges lined up. Place another tile on top and against the wall, and mark the cut line.

Tiles with Wide Joints

Some tiles, such as Mexican Saltillos, look best with very wide joints. For joints wider than ⅜ inch, use a grout bag rather than a grout float. Mix fairly stiff grout and load it into the bag. Squeeze the bag to control the flow of grout. Use the handle of a trowel or a dowel to smooth the joints. Allow to partially harden, then brush and wipe the joints.

❻ **Some outdoor tiles** can be straight-cut using a snap cutter, but many must be cut with a wet saw, and all notches should be cut with a wet saw. Set the tile against the fence, align the cut line with the blade, start the saw, check that water is running onto the blade, and push the tile into the blade.

❼ **Mix only as much grout as you can apply** in the time before it starts to harden. Using a laminated grout float, press the grout into the joints. Wipe in at least two directions at all points to completely fill the joints.

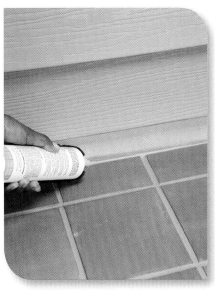

⑧ Tip the float up and use it as a squeegee to wipe away most of the waste. Run the float at an angle to the joint lines so it doesn't dig in.

⑨ Wipe the surface with a damp sponge. Continually rinse the sponge in clean water. Pay close attention to details, and work to make joints that are consistent in depth—just barely below the tile surface.

⑩ Wipe several times. Allow the grout to harden, then buff the surface with a clean cloth.

⑪ Apply caulk to the joints where the patio meets the house. Wait a few days, then apply grout sealer or masonry sealer to the entire surface.

TIP: AT THE EDGE

Thick, strong tiles like these can overhang the slab by an inch or more, but weaker tiles should stick out no more than a half inch.

Flagstone on Concrete

Flagstones that have been applied over concrete usually have joints filled with grout or mortar, giving the surface a more solid and permanent feel and making it easier to keep clean. Because they rest on a stable surface, you can use stones that are as thin as ¾ or even ½ inch—which will save a good deal of money compared to stones thick enough to be set in sand.

Choose stones that are reasonably flat and consistent in thickness. The more variable the thickness, the more often you will need to pick up just-laid stones and add or remove mortar under them in order to achieve a smooth surface.

Have a salesperson at a stone yard help you calculate your materials. Flagstones are sold by weight rather than size, so calculating square footage cost is sometimes more art than science.

You'll set the stones in regular mortar rather than thinset mortar. It comes in 60-pound bags that you mix with water. For the grout that fills the joints, you can simply use more of the same mortar. If you want a lighter gray color, use a mortar mix made with white Portland cement and white sand. If the joints are narrow, you can use reinforced sanded tile grout, which gives you more color options.

MATERIALS & TOOLS:

- Flagstones
- Mortar mix for setting stones
- Mortar mix or sanded grout for filling joints
- Wheelbarrow or masonry trough
- Shovel or hoe for mixing mortar
- Level or straightedge
- Wet saw, grinder, or brickset chisel for cutting tiles
- Notched trowel
- Rubber mallet
- Small sledge hammer
- Masonry sealer
- Grout float or grout bag
- Sponge

STEP-BY-STEP >>>

❶ **Dry-lay the pieces** out on the concrete, or on a sheet of plywood just to the side of the concrete. Aim to distribute different colors and sizes of stones more or less equally throughout the project. Try to have as few small pieces as possible. Cut stones as needed (see the next two steps). The narrower the grout lines, the more precise the fitting needs to be.

❷ **Where you cannot find a piece** that fits, lay a piece on top and mark for a cut. Once you have cut enough pieces for a 16-foot-square section, set the stones aside, preserving the pattern so you can lay them correctly in mortar.

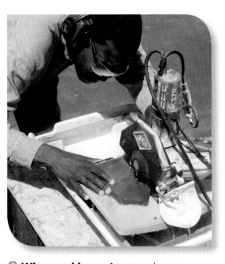

③ **When making cuts,** wear long clothing and protective eyewear. You can make straight cuts and some curved or corner cuts using a wet saw. For some cuts you'll be better off using a grinder or a chisel. In many cases, you'll need to finish the cut by whacking the stone with a small sledge. To achieve a natural look, tap all along the cut edge with a hammer.

④ **Pour half a bag or so of dry mortar** mix into a wheelbarrow or masonry trough, slowly add water, and mix with a shovel or hoe until the mortar is completely wet but stiff enough to maintain ridges. Shovel mortar onto the slab and use the flat side of a trowel to spread a ¾-inch-thick layer of mortar. Then comb the surface of the mortar with the notched side of the trowel.

TIP: PREPPING THE CONCRETE

The concrete surface must be solid. The stones will add only a small amount of strength; if the concrete buckles, the stones will crack. Follow the instructions on pages 166-67 for repairing a concrete slab. However, you don't have to get the slab as smooth as you would in preparation for tiles. You'll be spreading a thick layer of mortar, which can even out minor depressions and fill cracks.

⑤ **Lay the stones in the pattern** you dry-laid. Use a rubber mallet to bed stones in the mortar. Lay a 4-foot-long straight board or level across the surface to test for evenness. If a stone is too high, you may be able to press it down into alignment. If not, or if a stone is too low, pick it up and add or remove mortar as needed.

⑥ **Allow two days for the mortar to set.** Mix sanded grout or mortar. If the joints are narrow, as shown here, use a grout float to press the grout into the joints, then tilt it up to scrape away most of the excess. Wipe with a damp sponge, continually rinsing the sponge and changing the water, to fully clean the stones. Use the sponge to make joints that are all just slightly below the surface of the stones. Clean several times. If after a day you have grout haze on the stones, clean with vinegar. If that doesn't work, wear protective clothing and scrub with a mild muriatic solution—one part acid to three parts water.

TIP: GRAVEL INSTEAD OF MORTAR OR GROUT

Some large flagstones have wide gaps filled with gravel instead of mortar. This makes cleaning a bit more difficult—if you spray water with high pressure, the gravel stones will come out—but the look is most pleasing, and it saves you the trouble of filling joints with mortar or grout.

Stepping Stones

These stones nestle in the yard like islands in a sea of grass. At a stone yard or home center you can buy natural flagstones, at least 1½ inches thick, all nearly equal in size. Or use concrete pavers, generally circular or octagonal in shape; many are available with decorative surfaces.

A short pathway of stepping stones can be a great weekend project: attractive and useful, yet simple and inexpensive. Spend plenty of time arranging stones artfully, and you may make a charming backyard feature that will create a homey atmosphere more effectively than projects that are far more expensive.

MATERIALS & TOOLS:

- Stepping stones
- A bag or two of rough sand
- Chalk used for a chalkline
- Garden trowel
- Level or straightedge board
- Shovel
- Hoses and boards for trial layouts

STEP-BY-STEP >>>

❶ **Lay out the site** with hoses and boards to keep them basically parallel. Squirt chalkline chalk alongside the hoses to mark the perimeter.

❷ **Spread the stones** between the lines. Aim for an even distribution of larger and smaller stones. Enlist opinions of family members to achieve the most artful arrangement.

❸ **Once you are satisfied** with the arrangement, mark the outlines of the stones with chalk.

TIP: SPACING AND SIZING

If you make a single-file path with a single row of stepping stones, space them 8 to 10 inches apart. Where the path makes a turn, use stones about 1½ times larger than the average. Position stones so their shapes subtly mimic nearby stones.

④ **Remove the stones** and set them aside. Use a pointed shovel to slice along the lines and dig out the sod. Dig a hole as thick as the stone, plus 1 to 2 inches for the sand.

⑤ **Spread sand in the hole** and set the stone back in place. Stones should be just barely above ground level, so a lawn mower can run over them. Stand on the stones to make sure they are stable, and adjust the sand as needed. Check with a level or straight board to see that stones are at the same height.

Stepper Strategies

The project shown on these pages creates a sort of mini-patio with wide joints. Another strategy is to install a single row of steppers, positioned for easy walking. A line of stones running through a garden can be simply set atop the soil; then mulch up to the level of the stones. For a more elaborate installation, excavate and create a stable base for the stones, then add timber edging and fill in with gravel.

Stackable Retaining Wall

ere's an elegant way to solve the problem of a slope, or to create a garden bed. A number of manufacturers make concrete blocks that easily stack to form a retaining wall. The blocks have natural-looking facing sides. Commonly available colors include grays, browns, and reds.

A stackable wall effectively retains soil because the blocks have lips or other interlocking features that keep them tied together. When stacked, they automatically lean back toward the soil they will retain. Because the blocks are not mortared together, water can seep through the front of the wall, reducing pressure that can buckle a wall.

A wall like this works well as long as it's no more than 4 feet tall. If you need a taller wall to solve a serious landscaping problem, call in a professional.

MATERIALS & TOOLS:

- Stackable retaining wall blocks
- Capstones or blocks
- Compactible gravel
- Mason's line and stakes
- Construction adhesive
- Caulk gun
- Shovel
- Level
- Hand tamper
- Small sledge
- Rubber mallet
- Straight 2x4 for leveling
- Brickset chisel, grinder, or circular saw with a masonry blade

STEP-BY-STEP >>>

❶ **Drive stakes at each end** of the wall and stretch a mason's line (nylon string) parallel to the front of the wall. Use a square shovel to dig a trench along the line. For a 3- or 4-foot wall, dig a trench 6 inches deep.

❷ **The top of the gravel must be straight and even.** (Often that means making it level, but if the yard slopes gently along the length of the wall you may choose to make the wall consistently sloped.) Inside the trench, drive metal or wood stakes into the ground with their heads where the bottom of the first row of blocks will sit. Check for level or consistent slope using a level set atop a straight board.

3 Pour several inches of compactible gravel into the trench, then tamp firm using a hand tamper or a 4x4. Add more gravel and repeat until you reach the top of the stakes.

4 Use a straight 2x4 to level the top of the gravel so it is even and flat. Use a sawing motion as you bring the board forward and back.

5 Lay the bottom course of blocks. Check for slope along the length of the blocks using a long level, and check side-to-side using a short torpedo level. Tap the blocks with a rubber mallet as needed to achieve a perfectly straight bottom row.

6 Stack blocks with staggered joints. Most blocks lock together with no adhesive, but some manufacturers may require that you apply construction adhesive to each joint. Start every other course (horizontal row) with a half block to achieve the staggered pattern; this adds strength.

7 You may need to cut some blocks. One method is to score a line around the block with a brickset chisel and hammer, then break the stone along the scored line using a small sledge. Or use a grinder or a circular saw equipped with a masonry cutting blade. If you have a lot of cutting to do, rent a masonry cutoff saw.

8 For a finished look, top the wall with a capstone. The block manufacturer may make capstones. Or use concrete pavers or cut natural stone. Cut the stones and lay them on top. Then remove them one at a time, apply construction adhesive to the top of the block below, and replace the stone.

Freestanding Dry Stone Wall

A wall made by stacking stones, with little or no mortar to hold it together, adds a distinctive, endearing character to a yard. If built well, it can last for many decades.

Handling large stones is heavy work, but the design shown here does simplify the wall building process. Because there is no mortar, the wall is flexible—able to move up and down during frosts and thaws. That means that you don't have to pour a deep concrete footing, which is required for a mortared wall. And using roughly cut stones like the ones shown here greatly reduces the time you spend experimenting with different stacking arrangements.

Build your dry stone wall no taller than 42 inches; it will be difficult to make it stable.

Your stone retailer will help you choose nicely stackable stones of various sizes and have them delivered to the site.

MATERIALS & TOOLS:

- Compactible gravel (aggregate base or hardcore)
- Roughly cut stones that stack easily
- Gravel for the fill
- Mortar mix
- Field marking paint
- 1x2s, tape, and a level to create a batter guide (see step 6)
- Shovel
- Mason's line and stakes
- Hand tamper
- Hammer and brickset chisel
- Wet-cutting masonry cutoff saw (rented)

A dry stone wall rests on a tamped gravel base and is filled with rubble stones. It is wider at the bottom and stones are laid "one on top of two" for stability.

STEP-BY-STEP >>>

① **Mark for a base** that is 6 inches wider than the bottom of the wall. Pound stakes to indicate the corners, then pound more stakes and stretch mason's line to guide you as you use field marking paint to mark the excavation's perimeter.

② **Dig a trench 8 inches deep.** Scrape the bottom of the trench with a square shovel, and tamp the surface firm. Pour in 6 inches of compactible gravel, and tamp it as well.

③ **Check with a level or a straightedge** to make sure the gravel base forms an even and flat plane along its length and width—it can be level, or consistently sloped. Sort stones according to length and color so you can evenly distribute them. Save the largest and most attractive stones for the top course.

④ **At each end of the wall,** lay a bondstone—a stone long enough to stretch across the wall's width. Lay the first course of stones in two wythes (stacks). Leave space between the wythes. Every 4 to 6 feet, lay another bondstone.

⑤ **Cutting thick stones** by hand is very difficult, so rent a masonry cutoff saw. The one shown works like a wet-cutting tile saw. Another type is basically a very large circular saw that you use to cut freehand. Ask your stone dealer to recommend a saw for your stone. Once stones have been cut, use a hammer to tap along the cut edges that will be exposed, for a natural appearance.

TIP: STACKING RULES

- Position stones so they span the joint between the stones directly below (Follow the ancient masonic "one on top of two" rule: Each stone should span a joint between the stones it rests on, and no joint should be directly above another joint.

- As you build upward, the wall becomes narrower. The top of the wall should have the two wythes touching each other, with no visible gravel. To achieve this, experiment by stacking a short length of wall to make sure you start out with the correct width.

Freestanding Dry Stone Wall

(Continued from previous page)

⑥ As you lay more courses, "batter," or angle, them back toward the center of the wall. This is important for stability. Make a simple batter guide like the one shown using 1x2s, a level, and tape. The top of a 3-foot-long guide should be 3 inches wider than the bottom. When you hold the guide against the wall, it is correctly battered when the level indicates plumb.

⑦ After you've stacked several courses, fill the space between with gravel or stones.

⑧ For the top course, use as many bondstones as you can. Tip the stones slightly so rainwater can run off; you may need to insert small stones under them on one side. It's a good idea to set the top stones in a bed of mortar.

Dry Stone Retaining Wall

A retaining wall holds back soil on one side, solving slope problems and perhaps easing the task of gardening, since you don't have to bend low to reach the plants on the up side. The wall should be battered toward the soil that is being retained.

If the soil you want to retain is taller than 42 inches, don't try to hold it back with a single wall like this. Instead, build two or more walls to create steplike terraces.

Retaining walls can add greatly to the value of a sloping yard by leveling some of the landscape.

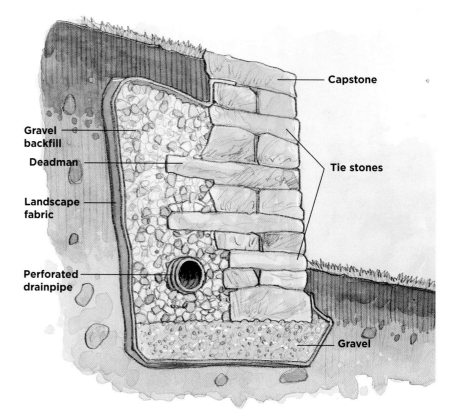

Capstone

Gravel backfill

Deadman

Landscape fabric

Perforated drainpipe

Tie stones

Gravel

A dry-stone retaining wall has plenty of openings for rainwater to seep through, so you don't have to worry about hydraulic pressure building up behind it. If you don't want water to come out the front of the wall, excavate an area about 16 inches behind the wall and add landscaping fabric as shown. As you build, add gravel behind the wall. Near the bottom, tun a plastic drain, sloped so it carries water in the direction you choose.

A Short Flagstone Wall

A flagstone wall presents a multitiered face, for a pleasantly jumbled look. It can function as a freestanding or a retaining wall.

If you buy wide flagstones, you can build in one wythe (stack). Thin stones are fairly light and can be easily shifted around to find the most artful and stable position.

Keep the wall no more than 3 feet high. You may choose to apply hidden mortar (recessed so it is not visible) to every other course for more stability. The mortar may crack with freezing winters, but even after cracking it will help keep the stones stable.

STEP-BY-STEP >>>

❶ Dig a trench 8 inches deep and 8 inches wider than the wall. Excavate either for a freestanding or a retaining wall. Scrape and tamp the trench so it is flat and even. Add 6 inches of loose gravel, and smooth with a flat shovel. Use a straight board to level the gravel.

❷ Lay the first course using the widest stones. For each succeeding course, use progressively narrower stones. Wherever possible stack stones that span across the width of the wall, but in some cases you will need to lay two smaller stones side by side.

❸ Dry-fit the top course in a pleasing pattern, then remove the stones and set them next to the wall so you know where they will go. Mix and apply a 2-inch layer of mortar on the next-to-last course and lay the top stones in the mortar.

Arbor

This attractive arbor has a classic design that makes it a welcome landscape addition. At about 48 inches wide and 32 inches deep, it is amply sized to span over a pathway. Or place it over a lawn chair in a garden corner to create a homey bower. The trellises on each side invite climbing vines to seek new heights.

Here we show building with pressure-treated lumber, then painting. For a bit more money, you could use cedar or redwood, either stained or unfinished to turn a silvery gray as it ages. Keep in mind that if you paint the arbor and then allow vines to grow onto it, repainting will be a bit difficult; plan to give it a long-lasting paint surface with generous coats of high-quality paint. Our strategy is to prime the pieces, build the arbor, then apply the finish paint.

For the posts, use treated lumber rated for "ground contact" or "in-ground" use. For all the parts that will be above the ground, less expensive lumber with an "above-ground" rating will do just fine.

An arbor is a casual structure, so it is common to sink the posts 2 to 3 feet into the ground and fill around with well tamped soil. If you want more stability, sink the posts 42 inches or so, and fill the hole around each post with poured concrete.

MATERIALS & TOOLS:

- Four 10-foot treated 3x3s or 4x4s for posts
- One 8-foot treated 2x10 for making two arches
- Four 8-foot treated pieces of 5/4 decking
- One 8-foot 2x6 for top braces
- One 8-foot treated 2x2
- Circular saw with rip guide (see step 1)
- Power nailer or hammer and finish nails
- Drill
- Trimhead screws
- Jigsaw
- Tape measure
- Carpenter's square and angle square
- Level and post level
- Post hole digger
- Primer and paint
- Paintbrush
- Drop cloth

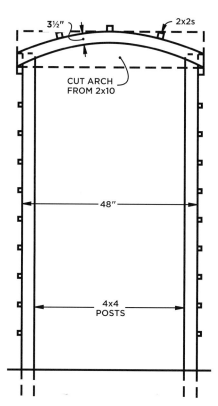

3½" 2x2s

CUT ARCH FROM 2x10

48"

4x4 POSTS

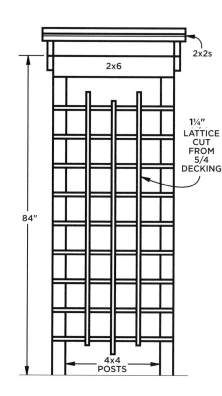

2x2s

2x6

1¼" LATTICE CUT FROM 5/4 DECKING

84"

4x4 POSTS

STEP-BY-STEP >>>

① **If you have a table saw,** use it to rip-cut the lattice pieces. However, for a rustic structure like an arbor, it's easy to produce straight-enough rips using a circular saw with a rip guide. Insert the guide into the slots in the saw's plate, measure from the blade to the guide, and tighten the setscrew.

② **Place the board to be ripped** (here, 5/4 decking) on a stable surface, supported every 2 or 3 feet. Adjust the saw's blade to cut about ¼ inch deeper than the board's thickness. Holding the rip guide against the side of the board, make long, smooth cuts; avoid starting and stopping.

③ **Once all the lattice pieces have been rip-cut,** cut them to length as determined by your design. To cut a number of pieces at once, clamp them together. Use an angle square as a guide to make a square cut through all the pieces.

④ **To make the arch,** mark a 2x10 for curves. Start with the top curve cut. Near each end, 3½ inches up from the bottom, drive a screw partway. Place a thin, flexible piece of wood below the screws, and push up in the middle until it reaches the top. Drive another screw to hold it in place at the top. Push up on the flexible piece midway between the screws, and drive two more screws to make a graceful curve.

⑤ **You can cut with a jigsaw;** just be sure to make smooth, sweeping strokes rather than constantly making small adjustments. Cutting with a circular saw is often a better option. You'll need to constantly turn the saw as you cut. Practice on scrap pieces, then cut the real thing once you've gained proficiency.

⑥ **Once the first cut is completed,** make a simple jig using a 3½-inch-long piece with a short piece attached to its end. Hold a pencil against the jig as you slide it along to produce a line that is consistently 3½ inches parallel to the first cut line. Cut this line as well.

Arbor

(Continued from previous page)

TIP: DEFEATING THE DRIED DRIPPIES

As you brush, paint will drip down the sides of the boards. Don't allow these dribbles to dry. Turn the boards frequently to brush away drips. First apply a thick coat to all four sides. Then, before it dries, wipe with a brush that is only lightly loaded with paint. Repeat until you've painted each side two or three times and you're sure all the surfaces have a smooth coat.

❼ Take a critical look at the arch you've cut. Use a belt sander to knock down any high spots and to round over the edges. Once you're happy with the arch, use it as a template to mark for the other arch, and cut that one as well.

❽ Cut all the pieces to length. Lay a drop cloth on the ground, and place scrap pieces on top. Position the arbor pieces on the scraps, and brush on primer.

Assembling the Arbor

❶ Lay two posts side by side, and place a cross brace at the top. Measure down from the brace to mark for the locations of the horizontal trellis pieces. Draw an "X" next to each line on the side where the piece will go.

❷ Spread the posts a brace's distance apart. Check for square using a framing square. Drive four nails or trimhead screws into each joint.

❸ Place the horizontal trellis pieces against the layout lines, covering the "X" marks. Drive two nails or trimhead screws into each joint.

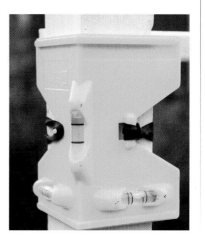
④ Measure to the center of the top horizontal trellis piece, and subtract half the width of a vertical trellis piece; mark this spot. Do the same at the bottom. Place the center vertical piece against the lines, and measure again to be sure it is centered. Drive a nail or screw to fasten at the top and bottom, then measure again and drive a nail in the center. Drive a fastener into each joint.

⑤ Use the same technique to measure for the other verticals, which are positioned halfway between the inside of the posts and the edge of the center vertical piece. Again, fasten first at the top and bottom, then measure and attach in the center, and finally attach at the other joints. Build the other trellis in the same way.

⑥ You can just measure according to your plan for the post hole locations, but it's easy to make a mistake. Position the post/trellis pieces and the arches as shown, and check that the assembly is

square. Drive a stake at the center of each hole location. Measure diagonally between the stakes; adjust so the distances are equal.

⑦ Use a post hole digger to dig holes to the desired depth. If you encounter a rock or a large root, try chopping or prying with the post hole digger. If that doesn't work, you may need to use a shovel or a long pry bar.

(Continued from previous page)

❽ Set the posts in the holes and check for level. You may need to dig some holes deeper, or lift up on a post and shovel dirt into a hole to raise one post. Have a helper hold the pieces fairly plumb while you drive first nails, then screws, to attach the arches to the tops of the posts. Check again for plumb, and make any needed adjustments.

❾ Add the top pieces. Place the topmost piece in the center, then measure and install the other two halfway between the topmost piece and the end of the arches. Drive two nails or screws into each joint. Check again for plumb.

❿ Shovel a foot or so of soil into the hole, and poke with a 1x2 to firmly tamp the soil. Repeat until you've reached the top. Continually check for plumb as you tamp, to make sure you don't push the arbor out of alignment.

TIP: POST-BOTTOM OPTIONS

• Mound the soil up so it slopes away from the post, allowing rainwater to flow away. Top the soil with pieces of sod.

• For a firmer foundation, you may instead choose to pour concrete into the hole around the post.

• In a moist climate, you may want to fill around the posts with gravel so water can drain away.

⓫ Apply two coats of finish paint to the project, working carefully to wipe away drips and runs.

Trellis

For the simplest trellis, buy a sheet of ready-made trellis material, build a simple frame of 2x2s, and fasten the trellis to the frame.

For a more custom look, plan carefully if you want all the squares in the grid to be square or equally rectangular. The surface grid can be constructed from 1x2s. The drawing at far right shows a typical plan. Keep in mind the width of the trellis pieces.

To attach a trellis to the side of a building, use hardware that holds it out an inch or two from the siding. This prevents water from collecting and damaging both the trellis and the house.

MATERIALS & TOOLS:

- 1x2 and 2x2 lumber
- Copper tubing and appropriate screws for your wall surface
- Pipe cutter or hacksaw
- Drill
- Saw

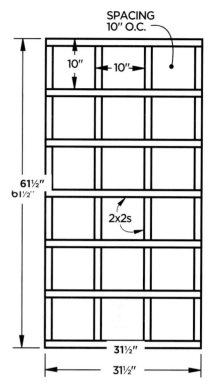

SPACING 10" O.C.
10"
10"
61½"
2x2s
31½"

STEP-BY-STEP >>>

❶ **Cut 1½-inch pieces of copper pipe** using a hacksaw or a pipe cutter: Place the cutter's wheel on the cut mark, tighten slightly, and rotate it one and a half turns. Tighten and rotate again, and repeat until the pipe is cut.

❷ **Drill pilot holes** through the trellis every 2 feet or so. Hold the trellis in position against the siding. If the house exterior is wood, position copper pipe and drive long decking screws through the holes and into the siding (see the next step). If the exterior is brick, drill with a masonry bit. Remove the trellis and drive the holes deeper.

❸ **Drive masonry screws** so they protrude several inches behind the trellis. Slip on a copper piece, insert the screw into the hole you drilled in your wall, and drive the screw tight.

Low-Voltage Yard Lights

A set of low-voltage outdoor lights can be installed in a couple of hours by a beginner with no particular expertise. Most lights simply get stabbed into the ground, the connections snap together, and the cord can be covered with a bit of mulch or buried in a shallow trench.

You will, however, need to have an outdoor electrical outlet nearby. If you don't have one, have an electrician install an outdoor outlet with an "in-use" cover to keep it dry.

You can buy lighting kits that include all of the lights, cable, and hardware and the transformer/timer. Alternatively, if you buy the components separately, you'll have more styles and colors to choose from, and you can mix things up with two or more types of lights. If you do this, add up the wattage of the lights you will use and choose a transformer/timer that can handle the load. For instance, seven 20-watt lights and six 18-watt lights add up to 248 watts, so a 250-watt transformer will be sufficient. If you think you may add more lights later, opt for a larger-capacity transformer.

There's a wide range of light options available, so take the time to choose lights that will really enhance your yard and complement your home's exterior.

MATERIALS & TOOLS:
- Low-voltage lights with cord and snap-on connectors
- Transformer/timer (may come as part of a kit with the lights)
- Screwdriver
- Drill
- Gardening trowel
- Pliers or wire strippers

STEP-BY-STEP >>>

❶ **To install the lights,** simply poke their stakes into the ground. If the soil is rocky or hard, make an incision with a gardening trowel and push the light's stake into the opening.

❷ **Attach the transformer/timer's mounting bracket** in a place that stays fairly dry and is out of traffic paths. Following the manufacturer's instructions, strip the ends of the cord and connect them to the transformer's terminals.

③ From the transformer, run the cord to the lights. Bury the cord or attach it to the house as needed so it will not get snagged by people or pets. Run the cord past the lights. Dig a shallow trench or cover the cord with mulch.

④ Each light has a short lead and a snap-on connector. To attach, position the two parts of the connector around the cord and snap together. The connector has small pins that pierce the cord's insulation and make electrical contact. If you cannot completely snap the connector by hand, use pliers.

⑤ Plug the transformer/timer into an outlet. You may choose to have the lights turn on automatically when it gets dark, or you can program a timer. Follow the manufacturer's instructions for programming.

⑥ Some models have a HI/LO switch to adjust for brightness. And some offer multiple settings for turning lights on and off. Consider these kinds of features as well as style when shopping for your low-voltage lighting system.

TIP: LIGHTS TO CHOOSE

Many path lights have shades to direct illumination downward, but some spread the light in a wider area than others. A well or spotlight can be swiveled to direct light upward to illuminate an interesting plant or architectural feature.

Low-Voltage Deck Lights

Whether you want to set a mood outdoors or simply light your way to the door, low-voltage lighting offers an easy, effective solution. As the illustration at right shows, you can put yard lights and deck lights on the same transformer/timer. Just be sure the total wattage does not exceed the wattage rating of the transformer. If you want to have deck lights and yard lights controlled differently—say, have the yard lights on a timer and the deck lights on a motion sensor—buy separate transformers, as well as a motion sensor switch.

Yard lights are often sold in kits that include the transformer and the lights, but deck lights are usually sold separately. Your retailer can help you select a transformer and lights that will be compatible. If you don't have a nearby electrical outlet for the transformer, hire an electrician to install one.

For a professional appearance, take time to bury or conceal your cable installation.

Transformer

Outdoor receptacle

Surface deck light

Stair riser light

Walkway light

MATERIALS & TOOLS:

- Deck lights, including post top lights, wall-mounted lights, recessed lights, and riser lights
- Transformer/timer
- Cable and connectors
- Wire staples
- Drill
- Jigsaw or keyhole saw

STEP-BY-STEP >>> Installing Deck Lights

❶ **Position the fixtures** you've chosen, securing them to surfaces as recommended by the manufacturer.

❷ **Mount a transformer** near an electrical outlet. Place the transformer where it can stay relatively dry, and install a protective cover on the receptacle (which should be GFCI protected) if there is not one already.

❸ Loosely run low-voltage cable from near the transformer and past the lights. This may involve drilling small holes for the cable.

❹ Connect the lights' leads to the cable. Use the snap connectors supplied by the manufacturer. Connect to the transformer, and test to see that the lights work.

❺ Fasten the cable securely to framing members with insulated cable staples that are rated for outdoor use. Draw the cable fairly taut, and drive a fastener every 16 inches or so.

STEP-BY-STEP >>> Installing a Stairway Riser Light

❶ Mark the outline of the fixture's box. The opening should be large enough for inserting the fixture, but small enough to be covered by the flange. Drill holes at the corners on the inside of the area to be cut out.

❷ Use a jigsaw or keyhole saw to cut the opening for the fixture.

❸ Thread the light's electrical lead through the opening, and drive screws to mount the box. Attach the cover.

Index

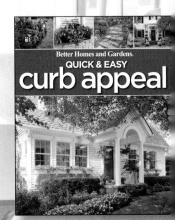
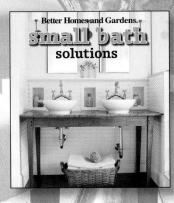
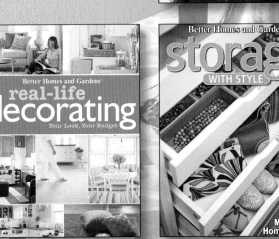
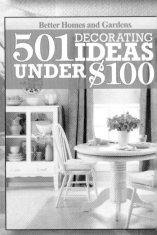